EX LIBRIS

מספרי

Walt Disney, in a film made in the fall of 1966, describes for the first time his revolutionary vision of an Experimental Prototype Community of Tomorrow. Behind him is an early layout of Epcot.

I don't believe there's a challenge anywhere in the world that's more important to people everywhere than finding solutions to the problems of our cities. But where do we begin; how do we start answering this great challenge?

Well, we're convinced we must start with the *public need*. And the need is not just for curing the old ills of old cities. We think the need is for starting from scratch on virgin land and building a *special kind* of new community.

We don't presume to know all the answers. In fact, we're counting on the cooperation of American industry to provide their best thinking during the planning and creation of our Experimental Prototype Community of Tomorrow.

So that's what Epcot is: an experimental prototype community that will always be in a state of becoming. It will never cease to be a living blueprint of the future. . . .

Walt Disney
1966

Walt Disney's
EPCOT Center

WALT DISNEY'S
EPCOT
CENTER

Creating
the New World
of Tomorrow

Text by Richard R. Beard

Harry N. Abrams, Inc.

Publishers, New York

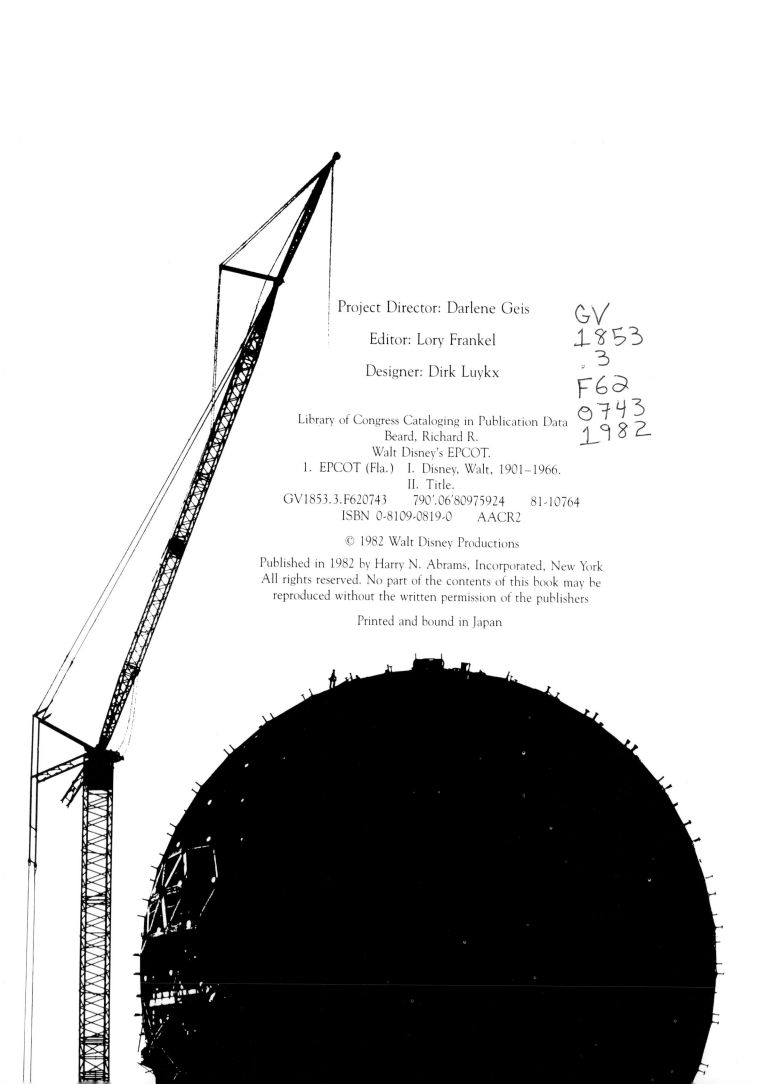

Project Director: Darlene Geis

Editor: Lory Frankel

Designer: Dirk Luykx

Library of Congress Cataloging in Publication Data
Beard, Richard R.
Walt Disney's EPCOT.
1. EPCOT (Fla.) I. Disney, Walt, 1901–1966.
II. Title.
GV1853.3.F620743   790'.06'80975924   81-10764
ISBN 0-8109-0819-0   AACR2

Contents

In the beginning was the plan: in 1966, Walt Disney and Card Walker (now chairman of Walt Disney Productions), surrounded by the 27,000 empty acres that will become Walt Disney World, including Epcot Center, study their blueprint for the future.

Introduction

It was one of those early summer days when the smog blankets the Los Angeles Basin, obscuring the hills that rise behind Burbank, Glendale, and other San Fernando Valley communities. The year was 1964. At WED (an acronym of Walter Elias Disney) Enterprises, the creative laboratory of Walt Disney Productions in Glendale, we had just completed the four Disney shows for the New York World's Fair.

Dick Irvine, then vice president of design for WED Enterprises—a post he had held since Walt Disney established his team to create Disneyland back in 1952—called me into his office. I was a staff writer in those days. Dick wanted me to put together some background information for a new project Walt had in mind. Dick described it briefly for me, in sketchy terms. Later, I realized that Walt had not really explained this new project to Dick in more than very broad brushstrokes; by getting me involved in what was really a research project, Dick was trying to anticipate Walt. He should have known better. In the same way that *Snow White and the Seven Dwarfs*—the first feature-length animated film—Disneyland, and so many other Disney firsts had developed, Walt had been thinking about this new project for years. *He* knew where we were going. *We* would find out in due time.

Two days later I was back in Dick Irvine's office with a name for Walt's new project. "Great," said Dick enthusiastically. "What do you think it should be called?"

"Waltopia," I said.

Although this name was created facetiously and never went farther than Dick Irvine's office, to me *Waltopia* is the essence of Epcot Center. Utopias are created by dreamers, and Walt Disney's dreams just happened to be bigger than those of all the other kids on the block and in his business. Utopian visions are seldom achieved, however. That this book is being published is testimony to another unique thing about Walt Disney: he was a *doer* as well as a dreamer.

Looking back, many who worked with Walt Disney see a logical progression in his life from his boyhood days in Marceline, Missouri, and Kansas City to Mickey Mouse, *Snow White*, Disneyland, the New York World's Fair, Walt Disney World, and now Epcot Center. Often, Walt "tested the water" before jumping in all the way. "The Old Mill," an eight-minute cartoon that won an Academy Award in 1937, was really the proving ground for the new multiplane camera Walt developed so that he could achieve new dimensions in the animation of *Snow White and the Seven Dwarfs*. The first Disney television special, shown at Christmas 1950, was a toe in the water which led to the Disney television hour. First broadcast in 1954, it is still on the air—the longest-running prime-time production on television. In retrospect, the four Disney New York World's Fair shows can be seen as stepping stones from Disneyland in California to Walt Disney World in Florida.

And Walt dropped little hints about his latest idea. John Hench, senior vice president of and chief designer for WED, recalls the day in the early 1960s when Walt stopped by his office,

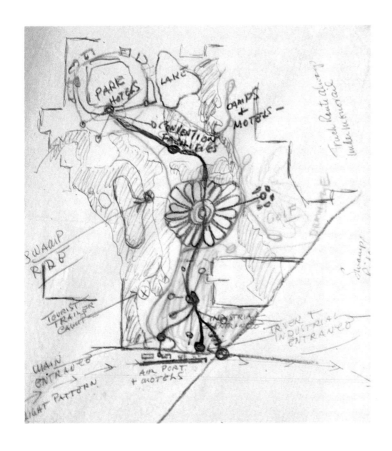

Disney's own early sketch at the left embodied many of the ideas that were adopted later in modified form as Walt Disney World became a reality. The rendering of Epcot Center, below, shows where each pavilion is located.

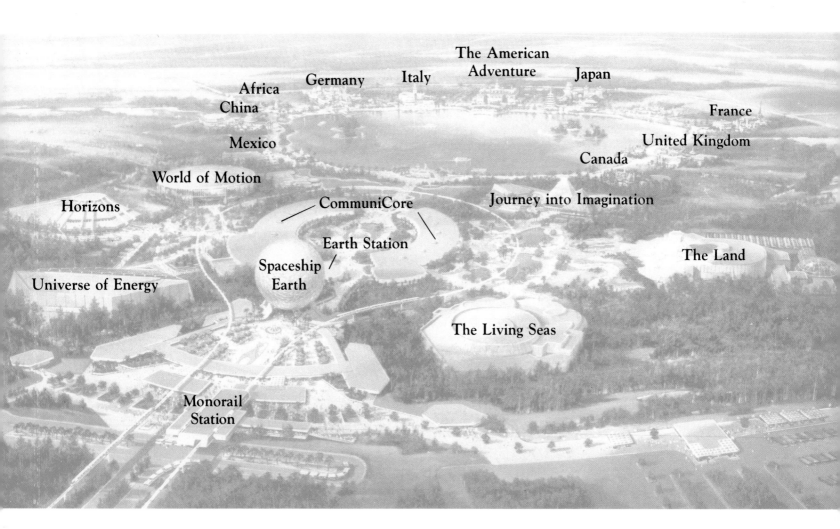

Africa
China
Germany
Italy
The American Adventure
Japan
France
Mexico
United Kingdom
Canada
World of Motion
Horizons
CommuniCore
Journey into Imagination
Earth Station
The Land
Spaceship Earth
Universe of Energy
The Living Seas
Monorail Station

poking his head in long enough to say, "Johnny, how would you like to work on the city of the future?" Without waiting for a response, his eyes twinkling, Walt was off down the hall, spreading more ideas and challenges along the way. He was the company's creative catalyst. As he told an interviewer from *National Geographic*: "You know, I was stumped one day when a little boy asked 'Do you draw Mickey Mouse?' I had to admit I do not draw anymore. 'Then you think up all the jokes and ideas?' 'No,' I said, 'I don't do that.' Finally, he looked at me and said, 'Mr. Disney, just what do you do?' 'Well,' I said, 'Sometimes I think of myself as a little bee. I go from one area of the studio to another and gather pollen and sort of stimulate everybody.' I guess that's the job I do."

How did the idea of Epcot develop? An article by Norma Lee Browning published in the *Chicago Sun-Times* on October 25, 1966—only seven weeks before Walt Disney died—outlined the project that was to be announced in detail in a scheduled press conference four months later. "You know, this is not a sudden thing with me," Walt explained. "I happen to be a kind of inquisitive guy and when I see things I don't like, I start thinking why do they have to be like this and how can I improve them."

That was the impetus behind Epcot and the "Disney World Project." Early in 1964, Walt gathered a small group at WED Enterprises and began to visualize early concepts for Walt Disney World, including Epcot: Experimental Prototype Community of Tomorrow. The words were carefully chosen. In a film whose script I wrote, Walt explained and recorded his concept in October, 1966:

Epcot will be an *experimental prototype community of tomorrow* that will take its cue from the new ideas and new technologies that are now emerging from the creative centers of American industry. It will be a community of tomorrow that will never be completed, but will always be introducing and testing and demonstrating new materials and systems. And Epcot will be a *showcase to the world* for the ingenuity and imagination of American free enterprise.

Walt Disney's death on December 15, 1966, was a critical event for the company he had founded in 1923 with his older brother, Roy. His vision of "a new Disney world" outside Orlando, Florida, especially his concept of Epcot, was so strongly a personal, life-summing statement that many believed the dream might die with Walt. Not so. For in addition to the fantasy empire Walt had created, he had also built a unique organization.

Roy Disney, Card Walker, Donn Tatum, Dick Irvine, John Hench, and "the two Joes"—retired Admiral Fowler and retired General Potter—were determined to carry out the plan Walt had outlined. They knew they could call upon the talents of the entire Disney organization, and that the organization was ready. Thus, when Walt died, the company went ahead with plans for the Florida project. Walt had said, "There's enough land here to hold all the ideas and plans we can possibly imagine." The first step was to establish a public focus...a place where people wanted to go to spend their vacations. To create these concepts was the responsibility of WED Enterprises.

Founded in 1952, WED was and is a reflection of its creator, Walter Elias Disney. It was WED's mission to give substance to Walt's ideas. WED's first task was to draw up a master plan, then to design the elements that went into the first theme park entertainment ever offered—Disneyland, which opened in 1955. Since then, WED produced, from the conception to the finishing touches, all of Disneyland's new attractions, and was responsible for its major expansions of the 1950s and early 1960s. By the time it was ten years old, the WED organization had been

Carved out of dense stands of pine and palmetto that surround it still, the Epcot Center construction site in Florida, left, demonstrates Walt's observation that "there's enough land here to hold all the ideas and plans we can possibly imagine."

Clear across the continent, at WED headquarters in Glendale, California, below, Imagineers work out their ideas for Epcot in paintings.

launched by Walt into new projects, including the creation of the Disney shows for the New York World's Fair in 1964–65. During this period, "Audio-Animatronics"—a new dimension in three-dimensional animation—emerged from the WED workshop. First used in such trend-setting attractions as the enchanted Tiki Room, Pirates of the Caribbean, and the Haunted Mansion in Disneyland, today they people the Disney theme park entertainment kingdoms in a variety of roles, visible representatives of the magical touch and technical skills of the Disney organization.

Creative resources unique in corporate America to the Disney organization, WED and its sister manufacturing and production organization, MAPO (whose name comes from *Mary Poppins,* the profitable Disney film in release at the time MAPO was formed), are composed of a permanent staff of designers, engineers, artists, writers,

Working on the master model at WED headquarters (foldout), two technicians add the finishing details to the plywood, paper, and cardboard model of Germany, scaled at ⅛″ to a foot. The smallest change in the design of a pavilion is incorporated into the model as it is decided upon. Italy is at the left, its Venetian campanile scarcely taller than a nearby paper cup. When built, the campanile will rise to a height of 100 feet.

In Florida, workers plant a palm tree in front of Spaceship Earth.

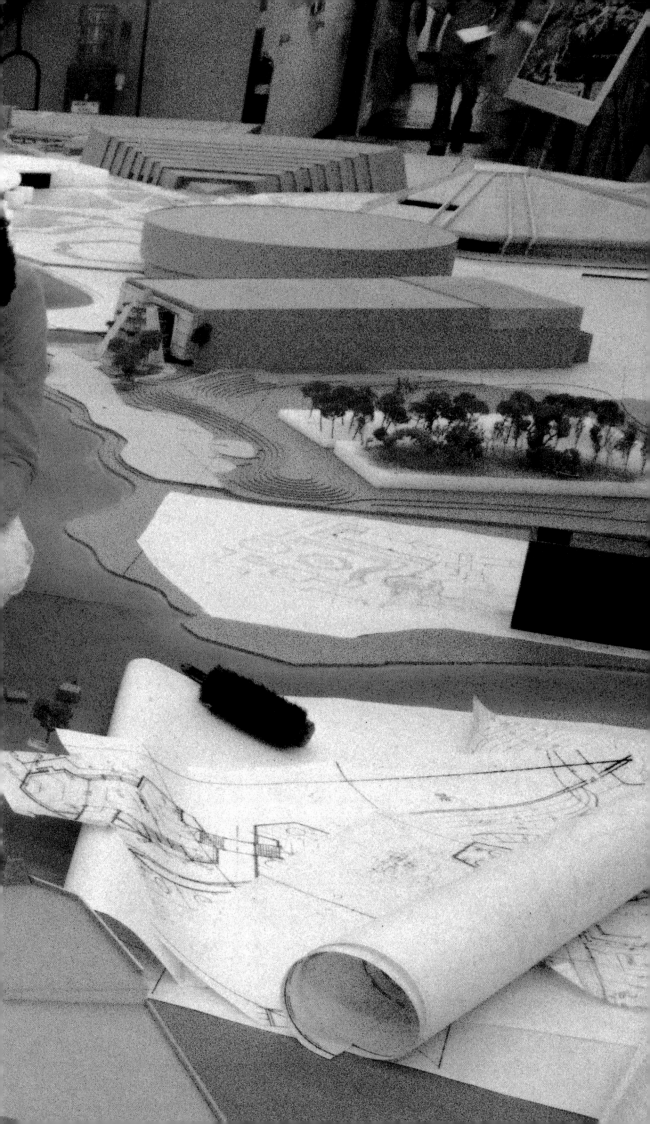

Working on the master model at WED headquarters (foldout), two technicians add the finishing details to the plywood, paper, and cardboard model of Germany, scaled at ⅛″ to a foot. The smallest change in the design of a pavilion is incorporated into the model as it is decided upon. Italy is at the left, its Venetian campanile scarcely taller than a nearby paper cup. When built, the campanile will rise to a height of 100 feet.

In Florida, workers plant a palm tree in front of Spaceship Earth.

architects, electronic and computer specialists, and many other talented people with dozens of craft and professional skills. Individually and collectively, they practice what we call "imagineering": the blending of creative imagination with technical know-how.

We consider ourselves entertainers, communicators, and, above all, problem-solvers, developing creative solutions that utilize state-of-the-art technology "to meet the needs of people," as Walt Disney often said. Out of our rather free-wheeling, informally structured environment have come such widely diverse innovations as:

- Audio-Animatronics®, the system blending sound with animation and electronics to create lifelike three-dimensional performing human and animal figures.

- The Walt Disney World monorail system, which has carried more than 300 million passengers 5 million passenger miles in near-perfect safety.

- The WEDWAY PeopleMover, a linear induction–powered transport system introduced at Walt Disney World, certified by the federal government for city use, and now in its first public transit use at the Houston Intercontinental Airport.

- The DACS Computer Central, which controls and monitors (from a central source) all aspects of show performances "onstage" throughout Walt Disney World, from the opening and closing of theater doors to the singing of bears and birds and the speeches of pirates and presidents.

It is precisely in this unique combination of creative imagination and technical virtuosity that WED has excelled. And in creating Epcot Center, we believe WED will achieve new dimensions and dynamics in family entertainment and learning experiences.

During the development of these new systems and concepts for Epcot Center, many media people, including Walter Cronkite and representatives of all three major television networks, visited WED. In 1980, Ed Prizer, publisher of *Orlando-land* magazine, described what he had found:

> Ideas and plans and designs and techniques and scripts conceived, reviewed, studied, endlessly tossed back and forth by teams of Imagineers, discarded, started again, refined, elaborated, developed into models and blueprints. A long, involved, never-ending process where nothing is ever final until the last possible moment—a process that only the men inside WED really understand. . . . I was to discover their unique way of working, individually and together. I was to get some insight into what kind of men they were—visionaries, perfectionists, workaholics. A breed apart, inheritors of the dream Walt Disney left behind at his death in 1966.

When, in July 1975, Walt Disney Productions announced it was moving forward with plans for Epcot, to some it was a bolt of lightning to

The semicircular structures of CommuniCore form the hub of Future World. Here
in this "community core" visitors can see and handle exhibits that give them an
entertaining glimpse of the future.

match the darting streaks that dance across the midsummer Florida landscape. The area had changed dramatically since 1967, when Walt Disney's film about Epcot was first shown to the State of Florida. Now Epcot would be developed against a much different background. No longer was the 27,400-acre Walt Disney World site—twice the size of Manhattan Island—virgin land with literally no amenities on its forty-three square miles. Now, nearly ten years later, there was a governing body called the Reedy Creek Improvement District, established and empowered by the State of Florida to adopt a comprehensive master plan, assure a safe environment, and regulate quality construction and maintenance. There was now the Epcot Building Code, clearly establishing Walt Disney's concept: "To provide the flexibility that will encourage American industry, through free enterprise, to introduce, test, and demonstrate new ideas, materials, and systems emerging now and in the future from the creative centers of industry." There was the whole Walt Disney World infrastructure that had been built in the intervening years: forty-three miles of winding drainage canals equipped with innovative flood control gates to maintain the flow and level of water; nine acres of underground corridors called "utilidors," a "city beneath a kingdom" that serves as an urban basement, providing vital operations and services—sewers, pipes, cables, workshops, garbage disposal—that keep the community aboveground running smoothly; revolutionary technical innovations such as the modular construction of hotel rooms, which are built on the ground and hoisted into place by crane; America's first all-electronic telephone system; the introduction in the United States of the Swedish AVAC trash disposal system, in which trash is funneled underground in pneumatic tubes to a central collection point; and many more forward-looking systems that will move urban technology into the twenty-first century.

The relevance of these developments to contemporary times has been noted by many visitors. In 1972, a year after Walt Disney World opened, David Brinkley told his "NBC Nightly News" audience, "It is the most imaginative and effective piece of urban planning in America. . . . We all remember seeing, years ago, those slick futuristic drawings saying what the future of the American city was going to be—gleaming buildings, fast monorails, people in one place, cars in another. Well, this is the future and none of it has happened. Nobody has done it but Disney."

For implementing these plans, the Disney organization has won many awards through the years. Few of these were so closely focused on city and community issues as the 1981 Award of Excellence presented by the Urban Land Institute to Walt Disney World/Reedy Creek Improvement District "in recognition of their sophisticated utilization of resources, innovative planning and construction techniques, beneficial impact on surrounding communities, and demonstration of the practical application of superior ingenuity."

As Peter Blake, editor and critic of architecture, design, and planning, wrote in the February 7, 1972, issue of New York Magazine, "The truth of the matter is that the only 'New Towns' of any significance built in this country since World War II are Disneyland in Anaheim, California, and Disney World in Orlando, Florida. Both are 'New,' both are 'Towns,' and both are staggeringly successful."

In the ten years beginning October 1, 1971, Walt Disney World's Magic Kingdom entertainment center has welcomed 126 million visitors, its attendance exceeding 13 million guests each year since 1976. These guests have come to the Vacation Kingdom destination resort from every state in America and more than 100 foreign lands. The theme resort hotels of Walt Disney World are so popular that they maintain more than 99 percent occupancy year-round. (They miss the magic 100 percent only because of closings for maintenance and refurbishing.) On peak summer days, more than 16,000 visitors stay overnight on the grounds of Walt Disney World in the Contemporary, Polynesian, and Golf resorts, the Fort Wilderness campground, and in the hotels of Lake Buena Vista adjacent to Walt Disney World Village.

Thus the planners, designers, engineers, and operators of Walt Disney World are already providing nearly all the public services of a city, from communications and security to waste disposal. Implemented by the Reedy Creek Improvement District, the Epcot Building Code, embodying Walt Disney's philosophy for Epcot, is firmly in place as the foundation for future development. What was lacking was a *public focus* for new ideas and concepts, a "center" for the communication of new possibilities for the future—directly to the public.

Nothing at Epcot Center is left to chance. All colors used in its many parts and pieces have been chosen and approved in advance. The WED artist above is matching the prescribed colors in his rendering of CommuniCore behind Spaceship Earth.

To answer this need, we are developing Epcot Center: a permanent world's fair of imagination, discovery, education, and exploration that combines the Disney entertainment and communications skills with the knowledge and predictions for the future of authorities from industry, the academic world, and the professions. Our goal is to inspire the visitors who come here, so that they will be turned on to the positive potential of the future and will want to participate in making the choices that will shape it. We believe that in a world where cynicism and negativism abound, there is another story, and we have chosen, with forethought and conviction, to tell it, and to be that voice of optimism.

Confident of our ability to entertain and communicate, in 1975 we began to form advisory boards of experts around the country to give us their critiques and add to our ideas for the stories of energy, transportation, the land, the sea, and other developmental concepts. To these men and women of science, industry, academia, government, and research foundations, we in the Disney organization owe a great debt of gratitude. Carl Hodges, Dan Aldrich, Chuck Lewis, Ralph Cummings, Tom Paine, Alex Haley, Gerard K. O'Neill, and many more helped point the way to a responsible, balanced, and honest exploration of our future world. These people found the time to help us despite their demanding schedules; many served without compensation, because they too have a vision of the future as a bright and better world.

The pages that follow will describe in detail how each of the pavilions in Future World and in World Showcase evolved. As you read, and as you visit Epcot Center, remember that at our opening in October 1982 we are just getting started—there's much more to come! And in measuring the success of our efforts, it may be helpful to judge whether we have achieved the following goals outlined by our chairman and chief executive, Card Walker, in an address to the Urban Land Institute on October 5, 1976:

- First, we want Epcot to be a *"demonstration and proving ground for prototype concepts"*... constantly testing and demonstrating practical applications of new concepts, ideas, and emerging technology from creative centers around the world.

- Second, we want Epcot to provide an *"ongoing forum of the future"* where the best creative thinking of industry, government, and academia is exchanged regarding practical solutions to the real needs of mankind.

- A third important objective we have established is for Epcot to be a *"communicator to the world,"* utilizing the growing spectrum of information transfer to bring new knowledge in the most effective ways to the world community.

- Last and possibly most important of all, we want Epcot to be *"a permanent international people-to-people exchange"*... advancing the cause of world understanding among its citizens.

Visitors to WED are struck by the enthusiasm and dedication of the talented crew working, often overtime, to create Epcot. Author and futurist Ray Bradbury, speaking to our staff, best expressed the strength of our motivation:

And so, really, what you are is Renaissance people. If ever there was a Renaissance organization, this is it. You haven't peaked yet, but you're peaking, and sometime in the next twenty years, when you peak completely, the whole world's going to be looking at you.

Buckminster Fuller lectures us on how to change the world and yet the only people I see who are successful at changing the world are right here—people with very special dreams. We're acting out what Albert Schweitzer often spoke of in his philosophies years ago. He said, "Set a good example for the world. If you are excellent, if you are of high quality, the world will imitate you."

What we're doing here is inventing a "Schweitzer Centrifuge"... that's the way I look at the Epcot project. If we build all this correctly, if we build it beautifully, if we set an example for the world, we can change the whole damn country. That's how important you are. That's how important I feel, working with you. People will come from all over the world; they're already doing it at Disneyland and Disney World... so, what we're going to do in the next year and the next five years and the next thirty years is change our own country, only for the better. And after that—the world.

It's a big project. But of all the groups in the world, while everyone else is busy talking, you're doing the stuff that's really going to count.

Martin A. Sklar
Vice President
Creative Development
WED Enterprises

November 20, 1981

FUTURE
WORLD

After Walt Disney World opened in 1971, David Brinkley called it ''the most imaginative and constructive piece of urban planning in America. . . . This is the future and . . . nobody has done it but Disney.'' One of the stops along the monorail that links Walt Disney World to Epcot Center is the Contemporary Resort Hotel. The entire Walt Disney World monorail system will have 14 miles of track when Epcot Center opens.

The gala wedding of history, technology, and entertainment, presented in a unique setting under the Florida sun, provides visitors with an unforgettable experience. The artist's rendering of the entrance to Epcot Center on the preceding pages says it all.

Whether you arrive by monorail or automobile, the entrance to Epcot Center is through the future. It is Future World that welcomes the visitor first, with the million-pound, 180-foot-high sphere of Spaceship Earth glinting in the sunlight, the largest structure of its kind in the world. Half a dozen pavilions form a wide ring around it, each dealing with an area of vital concern to all of us in the years ahead: energy, transportation, agriculture, mariculture, communications, technology—and imagination, without which advances in the other areas could not be made.

Every pavilion has its own sponsor and board of independent advisers, although the whole is coordinated by the large team at WED (Walter Elias Disney) Enterprises, the design and engineering unit of Walt Disney Productions, and put together at MAPO (named for *Mary Poppins*), its manufacturing and production unit. Each pavilion approaches its theme by giving us a look at where we were, where we are now, and what the possibilities for the future are.

The emphasis is on possibilities, since Walt Disney had an abiding faith in the ability of people to appreciate imagination and ingenuity, to recognize what was good. It was his contention, shared by his successors, that if people got the right information they would inevitably take the right action. The trick, of course, is to get people to sit still for the information. The organization that Walt fostered is a wizard at giving people facts they enjoy and remember.

Consequently, presentations vary from pavilion to pavilion. One show is dramatic, another leans more to the informative. A third is provocative, and a fourth is amusing. Some involve us as viewers, others invite our active participation. All, however, are entertaining, even while they lay before us the difficult and complex problems that face us in the world today.

At Epcot Center, the future is ever-evolving and fluid. While some pavilions leap forward fifty or one hundred years, others emphasize that the technology available to us today will create the world of tomorrow—indeed, that the world of tomorrow is already upon us.

Epcot Center itself provides a brilliant illustration of the use of forward-looking systems and planning. The monorail system could serve as a model of transportation for cities; waste material from the park, as well as from nearby cities and towns, will all be burned to provide energy at an innovative pyrolysis (incineration) plant that will operate twenty-four hours a day; and the vehicles used in the Universe of Energy pavilion, powered partly by solar receptors on the roof, will move about, negotiate curves, and reposition themselves all through sensors that respond to wires in the floors, charging their batteries by induction at specified points without any electrical connections.

Nor will Future World remain static. Several displays are designed to incorporate advances as they come of age, and additional pavilions are

Water hyacinths are grown in one-quarter-acre channels, in sewage water from the main wastewater treatment plant. The hyacinths not only thrive on this diet, they also purify the water. In the process, they extract most of the nutrient from the effluent. Twice a month, a certain number of hyacinths are removed and placed on a compost pad; eventually, this will be used as a soil supplement.

planned into Future World's future. Horizons, a look into the twenty-first century, is scheduled to open in 1983, and a year later The Living Seas will join the ring of pavilions. Not yet in the building stage are Life and Health, which will conduct visitors on a journey through the human body, and a space pavilion, to be realized with the cooperation of NASA, which will feature a simulated space station.

It is the wedding of history, technology, and entertainment, all displayed in a setting quite unlike any other, that makes Future World unique.

Disney's world of the future is realized at last under the Florida sun: Spaceship Earth and the monorail are key elements.

Each building has been designed to represent its theme in a style that is stunningly original while remaining appropriate to its subject. Behind each of these striking facades, where sheer fun accompanies the realistic and imaginative use of the technology of tomorrow, a new experience awaits us.

In the Universe of Energy pavilion, we "ride on sunshine" in a practical application of solar power. In the Land pavilion, a ride through a growing area permits us to witness firsthand the latest breakthroughs in agriculture. In Communi-Core, we are encouraged to press computer keys, push buttons, become personally involved in the latest available technology. Similar "hands-on" experiences are part of the fun in Journey into Imagination, where we can share in the creative process. In our course through Future World we will see many films, but they employ so many different techniques—including a dozen never before attempted—that after each film we will eagerly look forward to the next.

Enhancing the shows and rides are the startlingly lifelike Audio-Animatronics figures introduced in Disneyland and Walt Disney World. The "A-A figures," as they are called by their creators, are constructed of plastics in a Disney workshop. Outfitted with mechanisms that enable

The Mexico pavilion begins to take shape. At its entrance will be a waterfront restaurant and an imposing pyramid temple, which leads to the rest of the enclosed pavilion. The workmen here are watering the newly planted shrubbery. Across the lagoon, construction workers on the summit of Spaceship Earth prepare the framework to receive the final covering of aluminum "skin."

them to move convincingly down to the merest wrinkling of a brow, their faces and hands covered with realistic "skin," and their bodies clothed by the incomparable costume department in Disneyland, they are sometimes mistaken for the human beings or animals they represent. Their participation as "actors" in the various Future World presentations adds a touch of wonder to the audience's enjoyment and stamps the shows with the unmistakable Disney hallmark.

Parades and pageants, frequently keyed to special events and holidays, enliven the public areas and walkways. The world of tomorrow is presented in a gala atmosphere that transforms formidable technology into something we can understand and look forward to enjoying.

While entertainment will continue to be a highly visible attraction of Epcot Center, it is the underlying educational value of Future World that is its most important contribution. Exciting, amusing, and fascinating as each pavilion is in itself, it is but an element of a project that may well be viewed as a springboard to our discovery of new worlds.

Spaceship Earth

Presented by the Bell System

It is, among other things, the world's largest geodesic sphere—not dome, but sphere. It started out, less ambitiously, as a dome—the world's largest geodesic dome, at that—but, happily, the bolder vision prevailed.

Now the sphere, 180 feet in diameter, rises some eighteen stories high—a stunning silver ball dominating the landscape for miles around, with little to rival its rotund majesty. Although at first sight it looks like nothing so much as a gargantuan golf ball on the putting green of the gods, it takes on another aspect as we begin to appreciate its purpose—to reproduce the form of our spaceship, the planet Earth.

With an outside "skin" of an aluminum that is smoother than glass, the globe's facets reflect diffuse images as varied as its surroundings: by day, Spaceship Earth mirrors the sky, the land, the patterns made by Epcot Center's structures, walkways, and visitors; by night, it glints with the sparkle and illumination not only of World Showcase across the lagoon but also of the galaxies, the stars, the planets it emulates.

And if, on occasion, it reflects only a torrential rain, rest assured that the water cascading down the giant sphere will not drench the unsuspecting pedestrian below. The water will be collected within the globe itself, and be used to replenish the wells which in turn replenish the lagoon. Such is the way of Epcot Center.

Nor was the collection and recycling of rainwater the only—or even the major—problem faced by the designers of a Spaceship Earth. Consider, for example, the riddle of how to move some twenty enormous exhibition sets into such a structure—after the structure was built!

Epcot Center's engineering problems and solutions are as fascinating as the shows themselves. But many of the problems in building Spaceship Earth arose from the choice of a sphere as opposed to a dome, something that had never been done before. The concept stemmed from a desire to make a particularly dramatic entranceway, to give the effect of actually going up into Spaceship Earth rather than walking through a door in its side.

Once inside, we enter the realm of another team of designers, whose responsibility it was to create a show equal to the spectacular surroundings.

And so they did.

The theme show of Spaceship Earth treats of communications, a motif particularly appropriate not only to the pavilion's sponsor, the Bell System, but also to the Disney people, who consider themselves communicators above all. Specifically, the show presents the evolution of man's ability to communicate. For earliest man, it was a distinct advantage in assuring his survival. From a relatively elementary means of handing down lessons learned to generations yet unborn, communication developed into an increasingly sophisticated tool for sharing information over an increasingly large area, and for the transmission of history, culture, ideas. Finally, it has become an incredibly complex network through which information speeds, enabling mankind to share its accumulated knowledge for the common good, to maximize its potential for making wise and informed decisions for the future.

The story of communications transmits a message at once profound, provocative, and promising. In a "time station," before the show begins, a

Spaceship Earth at night becomes a work of art.

narration sets the stage: Who are we? Where did we come from? Left with the suggestion that the answers begin in our collective past, we board a "time machine"—an open train of two vehicles, four persons to a vehicle—to begin a trip spiraling upward through the great globe itself and sweeping through forty thousand years of recorded time.

Through a swirl of fog, light, and projected images that suggest another dimension, we perceive the figures of two Cro-Magnon men exchanging frantic verbal signals. In obvious danger from a charging hairy mammoth, their very lives depend upon the immediate exchange of information. One can imagine the crude but crucial conversation: "Watch out! He's coming from behind!"

A bond of survival formed, the two live to tell the story—and countless others, too. Now the vehicles move through the first of the ride's splendid sets: a cave dwelling.

Standing before a record, painted on the rock walls, of the wild animals encountered in the hunt, a remarkably lifelike Audio-Animatronics shaman tells tales to several rapt youngsters. By means of his stories he is conveying information important to *their* survival. A cave dweller mixes pigments as another paints a picture of a huge mammoth with curving tusks, while, in a thoroughly human vignette, a child who has been into the paint presses his palm print on the wall.

The next scene takes place thousands of years later: we are in ancient Egypt, riding past a pillared temple, where a man on a scaffold is also creating a record. This time, however, the message is carved in hieroglyphics, and the wall, of course, is manmade. (The continuing metaphor of "writing on the wall" is taken from an outline for the show written by science-fiction master Ray Bradbury.) Although the "writing" is again in pictures, it has by now become a far more elaborate and sophisticated system of picture script, or word-signs. So authentic is the Egyptian environment that surrounds us, the hieroglyphics can actually be read by anyone among us who is a scholar of the ancient language.

Beyond the temple, a pharaoh seated on a throne is dictating a "letter" to his scribe. His language and the sentences he speaks are true to his time and station, historically accurate to a remarkable degree. The scribe, surely one of history's first secretaries, writes with a stylus on papyrus in

An artist paints a model globe, right, to approximate the shiny facets of aluminum "skin" that will encase Spaceship Earth.

At Epcot Center, below, piles driven 185 feet deep support the powerful steel base on which Spaceship Earth rests. Visitors will go up into the globe from a central entrance underneath it.

The spectacular ride on a "time machine" that winds around and upward in the interior of Spaceship Earth takes visitors from the first images painted on cave walls, through the development of language and writing in ancient times, to Gutenberg's first printing press, on to the present marvels of television and motion pictures, and beyond to the future forms of communication. Every detail has been worked out, first with sketches, then with detailed small models and sets for the walk-through approximation of the full-sized ride.

a simplified cursive style of hieroglyphics, quicker, shorter, and more abstract than the version carved on the wall. It seems a natural progression in the history of communications, but actually it was a momentous step forward to take a small piece of wall, in effect, and make it portable.

With writing now a transportable phenomenon, we next make contact with the master transporters of their time, the Phoenicians. They had developed an alphabet of twenty-two symbols so simple that it put written communications within the capability of a greatly expanded segment of the educated population. Furthermore, while traveling about the Mediterranean from Africa to southern Europe in pursuit of trade, they were also carrying the alphabet to new places.

The set, beautifully rendered, shows two seafaring Phoenicians exchanging scrolls—and gossip —from boat to boat as their vessels, loaded with goods for barter, cross paths.

Our journey now leads us to ancient Greece, where the alphabet conceived by the Phoenicians had been rendered even more accessible. How? By adding vowels.

The Greeks with their vowels were able to enunciate their written word; they also elevated what has become the fine art of communication into the rarefied stratum of speculative thought, philosophy, with all its passion for logic and symmetry. Indeed, so smitten were they with the word that they gave birth to a dramatic form of communication that endures to this day; thus, the Greek tableau spotlights a small theater where a trio of Hellenic actors perform a scene from *Oedipus Rex* by Sophocles, a popular play of their time—and of ours. But here, in ancient Greece, the powerful words are declaimed in the very language of Sophocles and in the style of his day.

The Romans, who superseded the Greeks, in turn wrote a major chapter in the saga of communications. Organizers on a large scale, the Romans constructed a vast network of roads across the known world for the purpose of maintaining order

and establishing contact with the most distant outposts of their empire. Their primary purpose —to administer rather than to educate—was perhaps not altogether benign. Nevertheless, the result was a further spread of ideas, often to regions where the written word did not yet exist.

Such a communications network is suggested in the next scene, an elevated courtyard flanked by classic colonnades, where a Roman senator hands a message to a centurion with orders to rush the dispatch to Britain. In the distance is a street that branches into a system of routes, bringing home the converse of the axiom that all roads lead to Rome: insofar as communications are concerned, they lead away, too.

Eventually, Rome fell of its own excesses, but the art of communication was kept alive by the Moslems, whose Islamic empire surpassed the Romans' in size. While spreading the word, in Arabic of course, the Moslems received it, too. Discoveries and advances in medicine and astronomy, the decimal system, and paper-making were translated into a common language, then redistributed throughout a realm that at its peak extended from Spain to China.

The new network of knowledge nurtured vast libraries, one of which serves as a background for the next scene: we find ourselves in a handsome room where scholars are seated around a table discussing a treatise, while in an observatory tower, an astronomer with a quadrant probes the secrets of the heavens.

With reproduction of the written word such a laborious process, knowledge still was confined to an elite coterie of scholars. The tedious task of copying is illustrated in a representation of a medieval monastery in western Europe, where monks illuminate a manuscript by hand. The

Johann Gutenberg, the miraculous Audio-Animatronics figure at the left, is programmed to operate the printing press he invented. Here he is being fine-tuned so that his movements will be absolutely lifelike.

painstaking process results in works of beauty —and blinks of boredom: one of the good brothers has fallen asleep at his table.

Enter—and most dramatically—Johann Gutenberg, whose fifteenth-century printing press finally solves the problem of making information available to the masses. Pressmen insert paper, sort type, and work the press, while the inventor-editor himself, with a critical eye, holds up his magnifying glass to examine a finished page. (He will find little fault with the product, copied from Gutenberg's original Bible in 1981—and made with far less sweat.)

At last, books! And with them, a widespread kindling of the imagination, not only in the field of literature but in art, in music . . .

On one side of our vehicle we see a stern but benevolent Florentine schoolmaster reading Virgil to his students, reaching back to classical themes through "modern" methods. On the other side, in an artists' workshop of the Renaissance, sculptors sculpt while musicians play. Ahead and high above, working from a scaffold while lying on his back, Michelangelo, in a final, breathtaking tableau, paints the glorious fresco on the Sistine Chapel ceiling, before the explosion of inventions propels us into the present. Indeed, from this point on in the show, there is an illusion of speed (an illusion only; our vehicle is actually still traveling at a steady two feet per second) consonant with the incredible acceleration of progress in the field of communications.

Whereas the time span of earlier developments was measured in eons, then millennia, then hundreds of years, now our achievements are measured in intervals of fifty years, ten years, five, one . . .

We pass another printing press, this one a far cry from the early hand-operated device: it is powered by steam. The voice of a corner newsboy hawking his journals barely fades out before we encounter the miracle of Marconi's telegraph.

A local reporter in a nineteenth-century rail-

road station listens with wonderment as the telegraph operator translates an incoming message of mysterious clicks: "MAY - 10 - 1869 - OFFICIALS - OF - THE - TWO - RAILROADS - HAVE - GATHERED - AT - PROMONTORY - POINT. . . ."—yet another link of man to man.

Less than a decade later, Alexander Graham Bell successfully transmits the sounds of spoken words by means of an electric instrument: "Mr. Watson, come here; I want you." Ma Bell gives birth to a telephone system and an operator plugs into a switchboard of the 1880s, waits a moment,

Below is one of the many special effects that have been created to tell the story of communications in Spaceship Earth.

Michelangelo will be shown creating his powerful Adam on the ceiling of the Sistine Chapel—but first a Disney artist, right, has to paint the fresco. Meanwhile, opposite, an ancient Egyptian bas-relief is faithfully re-created by a twentieth-century artist at WED.

then utters a sentence that rivals Bell's for immortality: "The line is busy."

Meanwhile, scientists and inventors amplified the principle of the telegraph and came up with the radio. An engineer signals from a control booth to a group of actors whose audience—so far in space, time, and magnitude from the relative handful of Athenians gathered in that Greek amphitheater—now numbers in the millions.

Under a theater marquee we travel, past a cinema ticket booth, to the next innovation: on a giant movie screen in a theater, voice is wedded to picture in miraculous union.

Sound and picture are soon broadcast into our living rooms on small personal screens: a family gathered around the television set watches the favorite telecasts of the 1960s: "Ozzie and Harriet," "The Ed Sullivan Show," and Walter Cronkite's coverage of the decade's great events.

And abruptly the scene changes again.

For a moment, we get a glimpse of a thoroughly up-to-date communications center. People are running systems checks, calling up on a large terminal first a global view, then an electronic picture of the United States, then focusing in on central Florida.

We have entered the era of computers, machines that sort, store, sift, count; machines, the narrator reminds us, "whose billions of electronic pathways stretch to the very edge of space." We depart our trail through history and join them there, cruising into the dome at the top of Spaceship Earth, a vast planetarium where the heavens

are reproduced and some four thousand star effects might be shown.

From the vantage point of space we look back on the world—tiny, fragile, but very much alive, our own Spaceship Earth.

Beginning our descent—and passing on the way a crew of astronauts making repairs on a shuttle vehicle in outer space—we come down to earth, in more ways than one. We are, after all, fellow passengers on our Spaceship, and we are reminded that not only were the components of our intricate modern communications network created *by* us, they were also created *for* us.

Brief videotapes from around the globe demonstrate the practical, the human application of our advanced technology. They give a fleeting but telling impression: from bustling cities to remote islands, people's lives have been made healthier, happier, safer, more comfortable, and more pro-

ductive through the harnessing and dissemination of our collective knowledge.

With a last and rather awesome look at the current state of the art of communication—Landsat (satellites that survey earth resources) views of the earth; thermography; computer graphics and animation; microcircuitry; computer-enhanced images of ourselves and our environment; a veritable deluge of information—we ease gently back into our "time station."

Somewhat spent after the compression of forty thousand years into a fifteen-minute tour, we are nevertheless exhilarated by the prospect of another forty millennia, and rather inclined to agree with the narrator's conclusion:

"Ours is the age of knowledge, the age of choice and opportunity. Tomorrow's world approaches, so let us listen and learn, let us explore and question—and understand."

Inside the entrance to Spaceship Earth, visitors will be greeted by a towering mural of a communications satellite, left, depicting man's conquest of space in the service of transmitting information.

A sophisticated communications center is operated by lifelike Audio-Animatronics figures.

Earth Station

Presented by the Bell System

In a park of the magnitude of Epcot Center, it can happen to anybody:

You've just come out of Spaceship Earth, and where do you go from here? It's all so vast, even a little intimidating.

Or maybe you've just wandered into Earth Station from another pavilion, and anyway, wasn't this where you were supposed to meet the Johnsons? No, on second thought, that was at The American Adventure. But where *is* The American Adventure?

Or you're hungry and you sure wouldn't mind a taco. Somebody said they had them at the Mexico pavilion, but do they serve lunch there? And, more important, where are the restrooms?

For you, then, and for all of us who come unraveled from time to time, there is Earth Station.

Earth Station, also known as Epcot Center Information, is adjacent to Spaceship Earth. It functions in effect as Epcot's city hall, with a little Times Square razzmatazz thrown in just for fun—a Times Square that has been cleaned up and moved into the twenty-first century at one stroke.

It is the city hall in the sense that this is where you come to find out what you need to know about the community of Epcot. Beyond that, the facility replaces the "Tickets and Information" booths that are spaced so strategically throughout Disneyland and Walt Disney World and which, incidentally, dispense far more information than tickets.

At Earth Station, however, a number of those friendly people in the booths have been superseded by touch-sensitive video screens. It sounds forbidding, but even if you don't understand the first thing about computers, through curiosity, fascination, or maybe even out of desperation, you are going to walk up to one of those infernal machines, you are going to touch it in the appropriate place, and you are going to find out much of what you wanted to know. You'll test out all its capabilities, and pretty soon you're going to like it so much that you'll wish you had a computer in your own home. And who knows? Someday you may. Welcome to the twenty-first century!

What Epcot Center has done, without much fanfare, is to introduce you, innocently, gently, and entertainingly, to the new world of information, while never for a minute neglecting the human factor.

If you look up, you will see screens showing a quick-changing series of images, using a variety of media—photographs, films, animation. The display is a seven-part panel of 6 x 14-foot screens, each screen consisting of hundreds of squares an inch and a half across, each of which picks up and averages out its tiny area's colors from a rear-projected film. The overall effect is something like the masterwork of a Cubist painter gone Hollywood. While definitely utilitarian, at the same time the screens are a graphically striking means of setting the mood of the whole of Epcot Center itself. They fulfill the designers' desire to do something a little futuristic, something that had a little magic to it, something to convey the feeling that this is really a different kind of place, a special kind of place.

The three screens on the left are mirror images of the three on the right. Together, they give fifteen-second previews of the various pavilions—stylized, sometimes abstract interpretations of the essence of the shows to be seen at Future World

Replacing old-fashioned information booths, large video screens such as this one at Earth Station will give visitors a visual idea of what is available at Epcot that day. Visitors can request more specific information and make restaurant reservations at several touch-sensitive video screens.

What to do and where to go in Epcot Center? WorldKey Information Service answers your questions on touch-sensitive TV screens.

and World Showcase. The center screen carries information of daily or even of hourly interest.

From time to time, for emphasis on a special event, the pictures on the six peripheral screens fade down into the image on the center screen, where important and timely announcements are flashed: news of an astronaut's visit at three o'clock, for example, or a reminder of special entertainment scheduled at World Showcase. What you have at Earth Station is an overview of Epcot Center and its attractions presented in a unique, arresting, and wildly colorful new medium.

But to get back to matters of more personal import, suppose you want to know just how much a meal at the France pavilion's restaurant costs? Or how in the world do you locate a misplaced friend or a lost child? And while those large screens admittedly are mesmerizing, the bathroom emergency has lost none of its urgency. No problem. A bank of those touch-sensitive video screens is right in front of you, ready and eager to answer your questions, to solve your problems, to provide you with information literally at your fingertips.

Still, in spite of the spectacle of all those people eagerly poking at the weird but wonderful computerized video screens, you're not quite ready to put your intimate questions on view. You're not so much afraid as just a little shy. In any event, you might feel more comfortable communicating with people rather than machines.

The Epcot Center staff, anticipating this problem, has provided two guest-relations booths. To them, for example, one would go for special assistance for the handicapped; information on particular tours; tape players and cassettes that help the blind appreciate and enjoy the attractions of the Center. Here, too, non-English-speaking visitors will eventually be able to pick up headsets enabling them to hear show presentations in their native language. In 1983, translations into Spanish, French, and German will be available. The goal is to have a four-language capability at all of

Epcot Center's theater shows and ride-through attractions.

What about those computer terminals and screens at Earth Station? Will they operate in multiple languages? As a matter of fact, they are already equipped with Spanish and English, while French and German are on the way. The one language they *don't* use is computerese.

Your forefinger will turn on the touch-sensitive terminals whose screens operate by means of an invisible grid of photo diodes and photo detectors. This WorldKey Information Service, developed especially for Epcot Center by the Bell System, will smooth your path through the park—once you can tear yourself away from the remarkable new plaything.

It really is fun, and it works something like this:

On the screen, often superimposed over a picture, is a list of general topics; for example: Future World Attractions/ World Showcase Pavilions/ Restaurants/ Information on Epcot Center/Personal Assistance.

Hungry? You point to "Restaurants" printed on the screen. The screen then flashes another list: Location/ Food Type/ Prices/ Reservations. Once you have specified location and food type (in a matter of seconds), you touch the appropriate area of the screen, and a photograph or a video picture of the restaurant's interior appears, accompanied by the music played there. Another touch and a menu is displayed, perhaps over a picture of actual dishes available.

In the relative privacy of your own dialogue with the computer, you may decide that the prices are a bit beyond what you're prepared to spend. If that is the case, you can shop around (letting your fingers do the walking) for something more in your price range: the Farmers Market in the Land pavilion, perhaps, or a British pub lunch in the United Kingdom pavilion.

If, however, you've decided to treat yourself to haute cuisine, you touch the "Reservations" line of the French restaurant display. The terminal asks if you'd like to make a reservation. Yes? The terminal, equipped with an acoustic coupler, dials the central reservations office, from which a host or hostess, live on screen, welcomes you and takes your reservation: "Thank you, Mrs. Smith. You're confirmed for this evening at 7:30. Enjoy your meal."

It's possible, of course, that the French restaurant is booked up. In that case, you've saved yourself a trip, and you turn to Italian food, or Canadian, or whatever your next choice may be. This system, the designers explain, takes the reservations office out of the business of saying "no" to people. There will be some places—shows as well as restaurants—that will be 100 percent booked, but if people know that X is booked but places at Y are available, they reserve at Y. It turns a negative experience into a positive one.

And by having a live host on screen the human element is incorporated into the computer system. Another such area is that of Personal Assistance, familiarly referred to among the Epcot people as the Help Button. There are moments in everyone's life when even the beautiful simplicity of the video screen seems beyond one's capabilities. At such times, a single touch brings immediate assistance, live and in color. Moreover, the person on the screen quickly asks, "May I help you, sir?" or "May I help you, ma'am?"—at which point you just have to ask yourself, "Now how the deuce does he/she know I'm a sir/ma'am?"

Obviously, there is a two-way visual function here. The Help Button operates on the theory that in a time of emergency, great or small, there is no substitute for person-to-person contact. If your problem is not too serious, try to remember to smile: you're on Epcot camera!

This is only a brief account of a few of the functions of these remarkable terminals, which, in time, will be distributed conveniently throughout Epcot Center. At present there are a total of twenty-nine terminals throughout the park, some in Earth Station, some in kiosks, some in the Bell guest lounge, and others in the Communi-Core exhibit.

Visitors to Walt Disney World may be already familiar with the screens installed there as a prototype in 1981, while future visitors may also find them in hotel rooms and lobbies. At Epcot Center, it is no coincidence that most of the terminals are located where guests disembark from Spaceship Earth, a pavilion devoted to communications past, present, and future. The designers had suggested to the Bell System (sponsor of Spaceship Earth) a post-show exhibit that, in addition to showing what the company was doing, actually provided a service that people could use on the spot—something really vital to visitors here and now.

So the Earth Station terminals were developed. They are so attractive and easy to operate that you realize right away you don't have to take a course in computer programming to make computers work for you. In fact, once you become comfortable with the touch-sensitive screens and the other hands-on technology that is part of the Epcot Center experience, you won't be thinking "computer" at all. That's the real magic of it.

Universe of Energy

Presented by Exxon

The building, shaped like an enormous triangle with the apex tipped toward the ground, seems to rise out of the earth in a great swoop of silver and gray. With its unique architectural shapes and clean lines, it makes a dynamic statement, as well it should: it houses the Universe of Energy.

Among its more unusual features is the roof, laden with row upon row of photovoltaic cells, sparkling in the sun. These cells, 80,000 three-inch, wafer-shaped solar collectors, are arranged on the diagonal in 2,200 panels. All together, the photovoltaic cells capture power from the sun to generate about 77 kilowatts of DC current at peak sunlight conditions. This is converted to AC current to help run the pavilion's ride-through vehicles. They call it a "ride on sunshine," though Epcot designers are quick to point out that the cells supply only a small part of the energy needed to operate the facility.

Curiously, these photovoltaic cells were not even part of the original design concept. There were a number of early ideas, among them a solar dish, or a parabolic shape of some sort, that would concentrate energy into a superheated receptacle. Finally, it was decided to use solar cells. Besides adding another dimension of technology to the facility, the photovoltaic cells are so well integrated with the building that they add visual zest to the design.

In front of and separate from the main body of the pavilion stands a mirrored structure six stories high. The mirrors reflect the rippling water of a nearby pool, giving the impression of energy in constant motion. So, even before we enter Universe of Energy, we begin to experience the theme of the pavilion.

Once inside, we may wonder what we're in for, considering the critical and sometimes controversial nature of the subject. The very word "energy" conjures up, in most of us, anxiety over the future, coupled with boring images of industrial hardware and incomprehensible academic debate.

For these reasons, the show was designed to be entertaining as well as enlightening, to provoke interest and excitement while treating its subject with seriousness and respect. We are offered five individual experiences, each extraordinary in its own right, and each featuring film and show techniques never before attempted.

After entering the pavilion, we assemble in a pre-show area. Here, a spectacular multi-image presentation—live action and animation on a "magical" screen, accompanied by music—introduces us to the topic of energy with a review of its general principles. The screen and show were designed expressly for Epcot by the famed Czech filmmaker Emile Radok, now living in Canada.

The Radok screen, made up of one hundred revolving triangular panels, presents images in an intricate mosaic. Five projectors produce continuous images on the screen, which measures nearly ninety feet across. Each panel receives messages, via a servomotor, from a master computer, which is synchronized with the projected film. For further effect, each triangle has one side coated in nonreflective black and its other side coated in white. As directed by the computer, the panel can show a black or a white face, or it can revolve with its point forward to give one of several possible combinations of black and white. Almost limitless visual patterns can be created as images are projected in wavelike motions. The end result is a film presentation as dynamic as energy itself.

It begins with a vision of the universe opening up. An unobtrusive narration reminds us that energy

During the spectacular film on energy options of the future, the mammoth screen surrounds the audience with images of the space shuttle blasting off. In the inset above, a helicopter outfitted with a camera hovers above the thunderous Niagara Falls to capture, for the same movie, the awesome natural force of the cascading waters.

Visitors travel on a unique moving platform past a primeval swamp almost a tenth of a mile long, the domain of dinosaurs and other great prehistoric creatures. The ride ends with the spectacular geologic upheaval—earthquakes, volcanic eruptions, fierce energy storms—that folded fossil fuels deep into the earth.

Artist's renderings and models have been faithfully transformed into an actual journey through the primeval world.

is neither created nor destroyed, though it assumes different and important forms.

All the various forms of energy, in their basic states, are depicted in a spellbinding series of images. We see representations of nuclear energy, contained within the atoms of all matter, and of the chemical energy that binds atoms into molecules and crystals. Galaxies metamorphose into spirals, swirls, and crystals, and then into organic objects such as butterflies and roses, portraying chemical energy. Clouds meet in a zap of lightning to produce electrical energy. And next, mechanical, heat, and light energy are introduced, all through a succession of fleeting, sometimes disorienting, but ever compelling images. The screen's rippling panels intensify the phenomena pictured on it: water appears wetter, fire hotter.

Soon after, man comes on the scene and applies his ingenuity to the challenge of harnessing energy. He succeeds, at first using primitive methods, then more sophisticated means as he learns to release the energy from fossil fuels. It's a dramatic advance for civilization, but, "sooner or later," says the narrator, "present resources will not be sufficient for the world's energy needs."

A sobering thought, but one tempered by the promise of man's innate ingenuity—of which Radok's screen is a not unworthy example.

Leaving the pre-show area, we proceed to Theater I to see an animated film on the formation of the fossil fuels—coal and oil. Our theater seats are actually "traveling theater cars." These vehicles, each holding 97 passengers, for the most part "ride on sunshine" as they transport us through the Universe of Energy.

In making this animated film, the Disney staff was faced with an enormous task: to fill three screens covering an area 157 feet wide by 32 feet high. This film, thronged with colorful and surprising images—rain and lightning, volcanoes, tiny bugs and gigantic beasts—is the largest piece of animation ever created. For that matter, covering any one of the three screens would necessitate producing the largest piece of animation ever done! It was the director's mission to tell the story of the formation of fossil fuels while keeping the gigantic screen alive from top to bottom, from left to right —and in such a way that there is never a dull moment.

Despite the brevity of the film—incredibly, it lasts only about four minutes!—the size of the screen demanded scrupulous inking and drawing techniques that had all but disappeared from the animation industry. It was an art whose loss was much lamented by aficionados of the classic cartoons. They will be pleased to see its return here. Even the equipment had to be called out of retirement. A multiplane camera (invented by Ub Iwerks, the first to animate Mickey Mouse) was taken out of mothballs after twenty-five years and asked to do things it had never done before. Nonetheless, assisted by an animation crew of about fifty people, the camera performed remarkably. After all, the Disney empire was built on animation.

Even though the special effects are dazzling, we never lose sight of the story—how the oil, coal, and natural gas so important to our way of life came into being.

The film takes us back to the dawn of life:

sunlight gives rise to microscopic plants and myriads of tiny creatures that feed on the plants. Over the eons, a "silent snowfall" of organic matter drifts to the sea bottom and is compressed into shale or transformed into oil and gas.

On the land, meanwhile, plant life withers, decays, is covered by other layers, is compressed, and finally is transformed under pressure from peat into coal. Energy entrapment in fossil fuels happened over the course of millions and millions of

Created at WED headquarters in California, this tree and diorama are now housed in the handsome Universe of Energy, opposite page.

A sculptor makes a dental adjustment on Elasmosaurus, one of the monster dinosaurs that inhabited the seas over 70 million years ago. This care and accuracy result in awesomely realistic creatures that amaze the Universe of Energy audience, below.

years, but we are reminded at the close of the film that "much of the earth's present supply was deposited during the primeval era when great reptiles inhabited the land."

This ending acts as a perfect prelude to the next adventure—a journey through a fantastic primeval world. The doors of Theater I slide down into the floor, and our theater cars, now a train of vehicles, glide into the dark, damp ambience of the Mesozoic era—a world complete with swamplike sights, smells, and sounds.

This is probably the best primeval diorama ever built. The designers even used fossil references to make the foliage as authentic as possible. Indeed, page after poster-size page of blueprints indicates a painstaking effort at authenticity, right down to the leaf-scar patterns and needle clusters of the smallest sapling in the farthest clump of trees.

The ride traverses 275 million years and lasts only five minutes—though for the impressionable, the echo could last a lifetime. Here, in the dim and eerie setting of prehistory, we encounter the slithery sabalites, the towering araucari-oxylons, the squat and sinister bjuvia—and these are only the plants!

When we sight the fauna, our first impulse might be to retreat. Thanks to the uncanny accuracy of the Disney sculptors, the life breathed into the creatures by the Audio-Animatronics crew, and a boost from our imagination, we'll be convinced that the beasts have just emerged from a thawing

A terrifyingly accurate model of Pteranodon, one of the last of the giant flying prehistoric reptiles, will give the Universe of Energy ride some thrills and chills, while the hideous millipedes, below, should be good for a few shudders.

glacier, frisky and hungry after their long sleep through the millennia.

In a carboniferous forest, giant dragonflies flutter their wings, monstrous millipedes rear up to take our measure with their probing antennae. An edaphosaurus with a sharp spiny sail curving down its humpy back turns to glare as the vehicles glide into the main diorama.

It's dark in there, but as the sun rises we are reassured by the sight of a family of peaceful brontosauruses gathered at a pond. The baby of the clan plays with its mother's tail, and even when the father stretches his neck over the vehicles and spreads his jaws, the family scene holds little terror; we know they're vegetarians, and he is only chomping at the treetops.

This pastoral scene is darkened by a sudden rainstorm. A duck-billed trachadon arrives to inspect the vehicles full of intruders, but our attention is diverted to a fight to the finish between a towering allosaurus and an armored stegosaurus, the rocks teetering under their massive feet. We're conscious of a heightening tension as we roll through the mist, past a tidal pool sucking in a doomed elasmosaurus.

The smell of sulfur heralds the spectacular end of our voyage and signals the end of the dinosaurs' world. With a great rumble and heaving, a volcano erupts, pouring out a flood of molten lava that flows toward us in a bubbling, scarlet stream.

It's a finale in yet another sense—the end of a billion years of the formation of fossil fuels. So, armed with a concrete and vivid conception of just how long it took to create the fuel we have been consuming so prodigally, we travel into Theater II. Here, we are welcomed into the Epcot Energy Information Center, where seven video monitors highlight current and emerging energy systems from around the world. Then we are shown a mammoth live-action film that deals with our current use of fossil fuels and new energy possibilities, from bio-mass to nuclear fission and fusion.

Recognizing that the countries of the world are increasingly dependent on oil that frequently must be transported over long distances at great cost, the filmmakers have taken a realistic approach to the subject of energy availability and usage. Their treatment is both thought-provoking and optimistic.

As might be expected, the film is a pictorial marvel. It is projected on three screens, each 30 feet high and 74 feet wide, that curve around to create a range of vision of over 200 degrees, extending well beyond our peripheral vision. Specific story points are called to our attention through the use of window insets—one or more squares of film superimposed on the large three-screen picture.

In order to shoot for a picture of this magnitude, several technical difficulties had to be resolved. A major challenge was met with a Disney custom-designed camera rig—the only one of its kind built for this size screen. Less predictable was the problem caused by the camera rig's reaction to the frigid air of the North Sea, where the crew went to shoot an offshore oil platform—the camera sometimes froze in the extreme cold. The crew had to lug the cumbersome piece of equipment, which weighed over five hundred pounds, indoors to thaw it out before shooting could continue.

The twelve-minute-long film records the toil, sweat, and ingenuity required to obtain energy. But it is not without its breathtaking scenes of rare beauty—a broad stretch of the Alaskan frontier, the Middle Eastern desert, the treacherous sea. These images convey a sense of man's nobility as he struggles to maintain and improve his life with the help of energy.

Assembling Tyrannosaurus Rex, king of the dinosaurs, was no easy task for four strong men at WED. Machinery in his body will be programmed to make him thrash and roar.

Starting on a bright note, the film shows us solar panels in the desert as an example of alternative energy sources. "But," the narrator says, "the road to tomorrow's energy will be costly and take years to travel." The ensuing survey of energy prospects of today and tomorrow gives no promise of Utopia, but it ranges far and wide—even into outer space—to present us with the possibilities.

We see the old: oil drums in the Middle East, tankers pulling into the port of San Francisco, huge rigs at sea. We see "eye-in-the-sky" satellites, and "electronic ears" on land, helping to find new oil and gas deposits. We travel to the icy North Sea to see how drilling platforms—so immense they would "dwarf all but the world's tallest buildings"—plunge deep into the ocean to tap what was once totally inaccessible petroleum. We go to Prudhoe Bay, Alaska, to view the largest oil field in North America, and then we fly over miles of white wilderness along the route of the Trans-Alaska pipeline. We tunnel through dark mine shafts and skim surface mines to take a look at coal, a great natural resource for electrical energy.

And we see the new: we are introduced to synthetic energy sources developed from the pesty water hyacinth, the Canadian tar sands, and oil shale. Potential new sources of electrical energy such as hydropower, sea power, geothermal steam power, and wind power remind us that the forces of nature can also be tapped. Nuclear power is already an important energy source, but when scientists meet the challenge of fusing hydrogen isotopes at temperatures exceeding 180 million degrees to harness nuclear fusion, the process—safer and less expensive than fission—may generate an inexhaustible supply of energy.

The film then brings us home to point out the use of the solar panels on the roof of the very building we're in. It's a true and optimistic demonstration of how sun power can be tapped.

Our theater cars begin to move again and we glide back into Theater I. But now the room looks different. Curtains have been raised to expose fully mirrored walls on two sides of a triangular space. The ride vehicles face away from the screen, toward the junction of the two mirrors. In front of this is a large transparent scrim onto which images are projected from a camera atop the big screen, now behind us. The effect is of a 360-degree cinematic panorama.

The show, titled "The Universe of Energy," is a dynamic reprise of the concepts of energy we've just seen. This is, in fact, the largest computer-animated film ever to be projected. In a kinetic presentation, set to music, images—computer-animated line drawings, glowing in radiant, laser-like colors—melt into new images and engulf us.

It's a stirring finale to our journey through the pavilion, a finale of luminous color, flowing pictures, and lilting musical accompaniment. And as we leave, although we know the challenges are great, our spirits are lifted at the potentials and options that have been set before us in the Universe of Energy.

Not all of the thrills prepared for visitors to Energy take place in the age of fossil fuels. A modern oil rig in a stormy sea, above left, is about to receive help from a marine helicopter.

A technician in Special Effects, left, tests "molten lava," a harmless gelatinous material used in food additives to which orange dye and black-light pigment have been added for a fiery glow. The volcano will also shoot out appropriate sulfurous odors, courtesy of the WED "smellitzer."

Horizons

Presented by General Electric

The building that houses Horizons, like the future, can be interpreted in many ways. To some, it resembles a spaceship; to others, a finely cut jewel. This ambiguity was intentional on the part of the designers, who wanted a structure that looked like nothing anyone would recognize but that would gear the viewer's mind toward visions of the future. For that is the subject of Horizons.

Actually, it is a pavilion of the future in more ways than one: it will not open until October 1983. Still, its concepts will not be outmoded by then, for they are multilevel and far-seeing. Horizons is really a synthesis of everything in Future World, presenting elements of transportation, energy, food, communications, seas, all operating together to provide a better life for the people of the future.

Epcot Center's vision of the future is neither far-fetched nor forbidding. Significantly, it focuses less on technology than on a historically enduring social unit: the family. Rather than emphasizing the inevitable development and perfection of incredibly sophisticated machines of the future, Horizons concentrates on the purpose of the machines. And the purpose is us: how can our lives be enhanced by the future technology?

Getting there, as they say in the travel ads, is half the fun—except for that interminable wait in the airport lobby. In the case of Horizon's holding area, waiting there is half the fun.

It's called the FuturePort, Epcot Center's conception of the transportation terminal of the future, and from the moment we step inside, we feel the delicious anticipation of a pleasure trip.

On our way to the vehicle that will take us through Horizons, we will pass a departure loading gate where a status board and sound and light effects convey the impression of vehicles arriving and departing, an impression enhanced by the overhead public-address system. "Transcruiser now leaving for Colony Alpha; please proceed to gate thirty-eight," bawls the announcer. "Will the owner of a white hovercraft, vehicle number RM 34478, please contact the information desk."

Large octagonal picture windows—the future equivalent of today's travel posters—entice the tourist to visit the newest floating city in the Pacific, or a colony in outer space, or, nearer at hand, the last word in urban centers, bustling with activity.

While we are absorbing these glimpses into the future, in no time, it seems, our own journey is announced on the "Departures" screen, and we step into a four-person vehicle suspended from above. Looking down, we see nothing below. The vehicles make it possible to experience the sensation of floating free in space, easily and comfortably.

An on-board narration tells us, "We're on our way to the future, but we're really not the first. People have been doing it for centuries." Consequently, the first sequence of the show is called "Looking Back at Tomorrow."

We travel past still pictures of former conceptions of the future of flight: the Icarus legend; nineteenth-century renderings of flying machines; a man studying flight in a cage full of flying birds. Then, through a cloudlike frame, we see a Jules Verne spaceship, resembling nothing so much as a large bullet with portholes. It blasts off and flies into the eye of the Man in the Moon, leading to the next sequence: a stylized amalgamation of the late-nineteenth-century drawings of French futurist Albert Robida.

The model above shows the "mechanical wonders" envisioned fifty years ago: while a robot vacuums for him in the center of the room, the man at right reclines in a chair, having his hair cut and acquiring a remote-control suntan from the tropics.

The city of the future, below, provides a variety of ways to get around.

In Robida's conception of the Paris of 1950, long-distance travel is accomplished by means of large air-propelled cylinders he called *"les tubes,"* while dirigibles shaped like fish handle local transit.

The next set, splendid and somewhat nostalgic, represents the future visualized by Americans of the 1930s and 1940s, a future whose burdens would be lightened by labor-saving devices.

High up in an apartment building, a robot in butler's costume does the vacuuming. An older man, seated in an "automatic barber chair," gets not only a haircut but also an automatic shoeshine and a remote-control suntan—from Hawaii, the Bahamas, or Florida, depending on his whim.

While a woman in a bathtub watches a television set that resembles an old radio with a picture

"Looking Back at Tomorrow" presents ideas of the future held by people in the past. One such fantasy included robots doing the manual labor, at left.

The Neon City, below, will show clips from famous science-fiction films that deal with the future.

tube, another robot has run amok in the kitchen, spilling milk, flipping eggs against the wall, breaking dishes—indicating that perhaps the labor-saving era, with its problems of machinery going haywire, would not be such a Utopia after all.

The Neon City sets a background for early movie and television dreams of the future; in one sequence, apartments on bridges above crowded neighborhoods foretell one solution to overpopulation.

In this first part of the ride, the point is made that people have always looked to the future. Some of the things they dreamed about were remarkably accurate, but many of their fantasies were just for the fun of speculating. They didn't have the knowledge or the tools to make their predictions reality. The difference today is that we're learning so much about our world through science and technology that we now have the skills to build our future in many ways. The future is here.

With that in mind, we move into the Omnisphere, the segment of the ride that deals with the present. Here we are confronted with two Omni-Max screens, each eight stories high and eight stories wide. Screens like these are already in use elsewhere, but at Epcot Center for the first time every viewer will be placed at the vantage point, or "optimum spot," at the center of the screen. This will give the impression of being completely surrounded by film, creating a mysterious and awesome environment. It is the perfect medium to engulf us in the wonders of modern science and technology. Among the images planned for the Omnisphere are:

- astronauts practicing construction techniques for outer space in the natural buoyancy of a NASA tank on earth;

- the historic blast-off of the space shuttle;

- a computerized Landsat view of agricultural areas;

The Omnisphere theaters, in small-scale models above, will present larger-than-life scenes from modern science and technology. The screen is designed to curve over and above the audience as in a planetarium, and as visitors ride through the theaters, they will be engulfed in the wonders depicted all about them.

- a weather-monitoring station and a voyage through the clouds of a violent storm;

- a thermal cityscape changing shape and hue as infrared scans reveal invisible heat patterns;

- a thermal body scan, whose colored patterns reveal potential health problems;

- laser surgery;

- robots at work in manufacturing;

- a beautiful growing crystal;

- a "flight" over a microscopic computer chip, highly magnified to reveal its intricate architecture;

- a voyage through an unfolding deoxyribonucleic acid (DNA) chain;

- the Very Large Array (VLA) radio telescopes scanning our active universe;

- divers exploring our aquatic frontier in ultra-modern suits.

A narration explains what we are seeing, then asks rhetorically how all this applies to a future that is "just around the corner."

Literally around the corner, we come upon an urban living complex and meet the narrator, an Audio-Animatronics figure playing a theremin-like organ in his living room while his dog howls beside him. The sight of the narrator and his wife reassures us that there will be far better health care in the future; although they are both in their mid-sixties, they are very youthful-looking. She is talking to their daughter by means of a three-dimensional holographic televiewer. We can see that the daughter is speaking from a desert farm. In contrast, the older couple's picture window reveals a city of the future, where "mag-lev" (for magnetic levitation) trains reminiscent of those we have seen in the FuturePort zoom past. Floating just above the rails by magnetic force, these trains travel at far greater speeds than conventional trains and, because of the absence of friction, with considerable saving of energy. The implication is that no matter how great a distance separates the members of the family, they are only minutes away from one another.

Turning another corner, we enter the desert farm and see the daughter, who is directing the work of robot harvesters in the background. Her husband is in the kitchen of their nearby dwelling, tending to a son. With his mischievous son's dubious help, he is making a birthday cake. The oversize fruits and vegetables stored on a kitchen shelf, the narrator tells us, are among the fruits of genetic engineering.

In the family room, we meet the daughter of the farm couple. She is supposed to be doing her geometry homework on a home computer, but instead she is talking to her boyfriend by holo-graphic telephone—an example of "the more it changes, the more it's the same." The young man, who works on a floating-city project in the Pacific, promises to "come to the party," although he may be late—a recurring gag as the story progresses.

In a natural transition, we next visit his submarine workshop; this time, we see the girl on a tele-view screen. Among other marvels of the floating city and its environs is a class of fearless four-year-old children learning to scuba-dive. In the submerged portion of a floating resort, we catch glimpses of an undersea restaurant. Then we enter an underwater working area. At surface level, there is kelp farming, which provides both food and fuel. On the bottom of the sea a robot harvester "vacuums" manganese-rich nodules from the sea floor.

In a dark tunnel, we make the transition to the next scene as the twinkling eyes of fish become stars in outer space. We find ourselves in the center of a spherical space colony, which revolves for gravitational reasons. To create it, the Epcot designers constructed a miniature spherical set, then photographed it from the center. It is complete with residences, roads, lakes, even an illuminated sports stadium, all visible in the distance.

Gravity is zero in the center of the colony, of course, a fact that becomes evident as we arrive at a health-and-recreation center. In the background, a zero-gravity basketball game is simulated with players and ball drifting weightlessly; in the foreground, a physical-fitness buff exercises on a cycling machine complete with simulated sights and sounds from a street on Earth, and a man who is doing calisthenics gets a simultaneous automated medical checkup.

In a nearby docking port, a family arriving in

In the underwater city of tomorrow, left, man, machine, and marine life coexist in peace. Above, a designer works on a model of the underwater observation tube for the floating-city sequence.

space for the first time is disoriented by the lack of gravity; the distracted parents hastily grab their luggage before it floats away, and a weightless child and a dog also have to be retrieved.

One of the motives for colonizing space is to develop new industries that will produce materials superior to similar items manufactured on Earth. The manufacture of crystals, which can be grown larger and purer in space, is one of the most promising space industries. We are shown its possibilities in a scene of a zero-gravity "crystal farm." Robotic arms harvest the crop, opening the growing pods and moving the exposed crystal into the path of a laser defractometer, which analyzes the purity of the crystal. A scientist, freed from her manual work by the use of robots, checks the analysis of a very large crystal.

Down on Earth again, the extended family we have become familiar with is gathered at last to enjoy the party for which the cake was being prepared. At any rate, most of them are there: the boyfriend who was late never did make it,

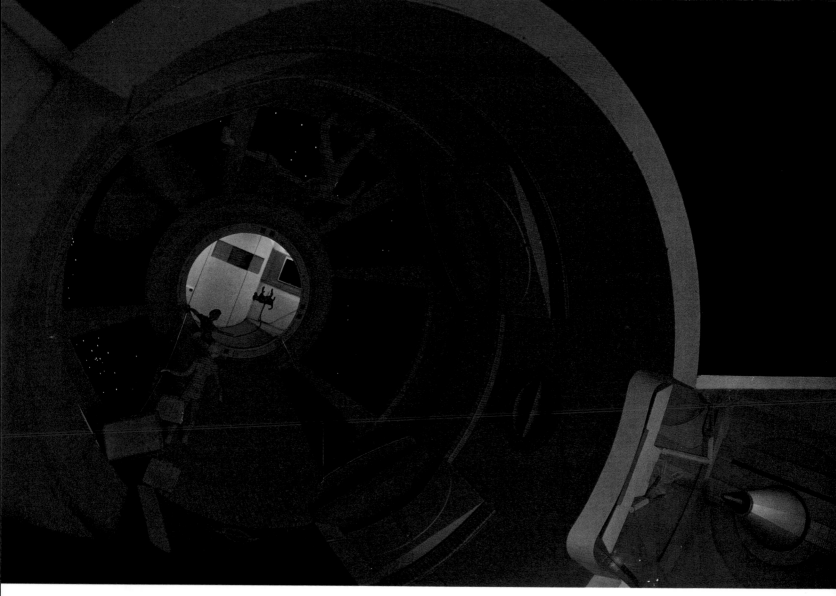

A family arriving at the docking port of a space colony is nonplussed by the effects of zero gravity.

although—another future boon—he is at least present in holographic reproduction.

We enter a "launch tube" and blast out into space, on our way back to Earth, with one more surprise in store. For the trip home, our narrator offers us a choice among four of the transportation systems we have seen along our journey: a "mag-lev" train ride through an urban center, an exciting race in a personal submarine, a hovercraft trip through the canyonlands near the desert farm, or a space flight through the colony belt. This is the first time that guests on a Disney ride will be given the opportunity to choose their own ending to the show. Through the use of touch-sensitive panels in the ride vehicle, the riders'

votes will be entered into a computer and passed along to the simulation equipment. Vehicle tilt, special sound effects, and high-speed simulations will combine to create an experience unlike anything visitors have had before.

Having voted for our preferences, we will enjoy the rest of the ride in our chosen conveyance. Our arrival is announced over the PA system back at the FuturePort.

As we leave the pavilion, we pass a colorful mural that encapsulates the whole show. It will certainly lead us to think back on all we have experienced in the pavilion, and to join our private visions of the future with those we have seen.

The newly arrived family will live in a space habitat like the one shown above.
Below is an appealing vision of a future city.

A busy space shuttle, pictured on the following pages, services the network of
communications in space.

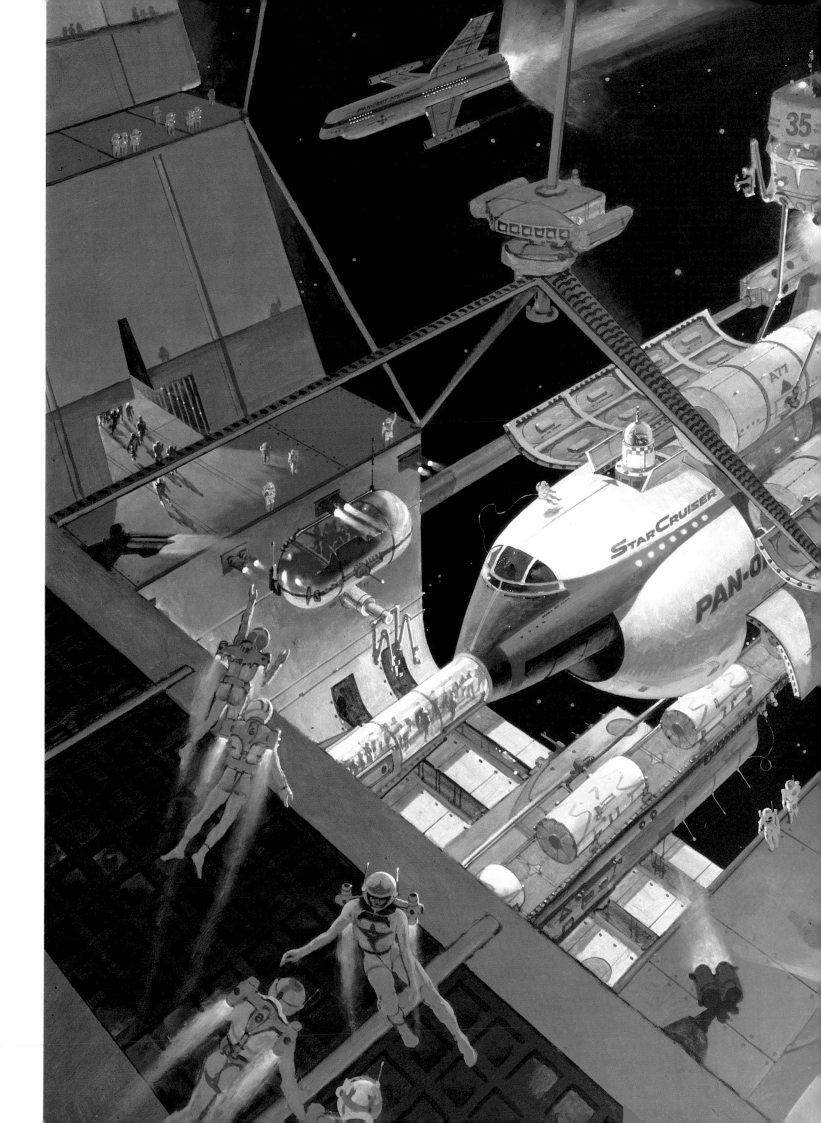

World of Motion

Presented by General Motors

Within the wheel-shaped World of Motion, the history of transportation is amusingly presented and the latest developments in locomotion are exhibited.

Unlike the angular structures housing Universe of Energy and Horizons, which seem to stretch into the sky, their neighbor is sleek and circular. With its perfectly cylindrical form, it may remind us of a wheel, which is appropriate to a building that contains the World of Motion.

While the structure is firmly anchored to the ground, the show inside takes off in many directions. On the ground floor is the TransCenter, designed by General Motors, displaying examples of innovative and advanced concepts for present and future directions in transportation. Between the second and first floors, the CenterCore, a stunning evocation of a city of the future, uses the entire height of the building—sixty feet. Starting our tour on the second floor, we ride through a show that presents a refreshingly zany history of transportation—including its low as well as its high points.

The history of transportation show itself may not gleam (the shiny new chariots designed for the "used-chariot lot" were beaten up to look properly broken-down), but its production is impeccable. One hundred and seven Audio-Animatronics people, 73 animals, 33 animated props, 16 automobiles, assorted trains and planes, bicycles and balloons, rickshaws and riverboats mill about in no fewer than 23 full-scale stage sets, each accurate down to the last detail.

The ride's theme song, "It's Fun to Be Free," begins in the waiting area, and so does the fun. From behind comes the sound of a distant steam locomotive. Closer and closer it chugs, until the sound passes over our heads with a hiss and a roar. Then we are assaulted by the clang of a fire engine, the clatter of an early Oldsmobile, and finally the roar of a jet plane, each vehicle accompanied by appropriately wacky music.

We board our vehicles, each car fitted with two benches, each bench seating three people, and set out to learn the unbelievable but true story of transportation.

In a pitch-dark tunnel, we hear mysterious footsteps squelching alongside our vehicle. Human footprints begin to appear, step by step, illuminated from below. These footprints are not only mysterious but also confused—one set of prints crosses over the top of the tunnel. "In the beginning," explains the recorded narration, "there was foot power." Leaving a couple of early *Homo sapiens* fanning their tired feet after their long journey, we begin to see how humans sought relief for their foot-sore travel. First we pass through a scene of early water transportation: a pair of primitive men float along on a wooden raft, oblivious to an attentive alligator.

Early man experimented with many ways to cover long distances with the least wear and tear on his own body. When he was near a waterway, the solution was relatively simple: find or build something to float on.

But land transportation was more difficult. In the first full-scale set we see an Assyrian tableau, which introduces animal power—not only camels, but also ostriches and zebras. In his desperate search for something to replace foot power, man tried a number of unlikely creatures. He even went so far as to dream up a magic carpet, a preview of future air travel.

In case we wondered how the wheel came to be invented, we find out in the next scene. In a Babylonian throne room, each of three hopeful inventors, clutching his own idea of the wheel, tries to persuade the king he has the ultimate solution. The one with the circular wheel wins this round over the rejected square and triangle.

In quick succession, we take a psychedelic trip in mixed media through a wheel factory (round ones by now), and pass Egyptian, Chinese, and Greek temples to arrive at a used-chariot lot in ancient Rome. There among old chariots is the Trojan Horse, up for sale in spite of being a little the worse for wear. A centaur, man and vehicle in one tidy package, also bears a "for sale" sign.

The Trojan Horse, slightly the worse for wear, is among the offerings in a used-chariot lot in ancient Rome, according to the zany history of transportation show.

In the next sequence, fifteenth-century sailing ships float on layers of undulating waves. Then we are given an exclusive peek into Leonardo da Vinci's studio. Mona Lisa, neglected by the artist in favor of his experiments, scowls while a

The history of transportation show gives us a peek into the studio of Leonardo da Vinci where we see the model for the Mona Lisa sulking while Leonardo temporarily abandons her portrait to experiment with flight.

The pig below is readied for its trip in a balloon, above, which heralds the "Age of Flight."

hapless assistant of the artist-inventor flaps precariously from a flying contraption of Leonardo's that didn't quite get off the ground. A true Renaissance man, Leonardo's interests go far beyond his time.

The "Age of Flight" is heralded by an intrepid balloonist soaring over the rooftops of London, a cargo of pigs, goats, and chickens peering over the edge of the gondola. Steam power is represented by a puffing steam carriage and a nostalgic Mississippi riverboat scene. A parade of stagecoaches and buckboards leads the westward movement, although this particular parade is stuck in a groove: Indians chase cavalry troops who chase the Indians, in an endless circle.

"Finally, the steam railroads," announces the narrator, "dependable, fast, and safe transportation." The site is the high Sierras and the train is authentic down to the last lubricator and injector. But bandits hold up the train, giving the passengers an unscheduled diversion and giving the lie to one-third of the narrator's description.

"The world's first traffic jam" is a surpassingly glorious mess. In the main square of an American city of around 1910, a horse-drawn produce cart has tangled with a fruit peddler, with predictable results. The street is strewn with vegetables and fruit, the round ones rolling crazily, the others crushed to a messy pulp. Backed up behind the wreckage are all manner of conveyances: a double-deck bus, an ice truck, a junk wagon, one of the

Guided by the small model in the foreground, designers, below, work on the full-scale set for a classic traffic jam in an early twentieth-century American city. Above, a frustrated Audio-Animatronics motorist caught in the commotion is placed in his vehicle.

TransCenter, on the ground floor of World of Motion, was designed by General Motors and features exciting hands-on displays of automotive science.

new-fangled horseless carriages. A classic cacaphony fills the square: kids yelling, cops whistling, horns honking, motors backfiring, and from an upstairs window a piano tinkling the syncopated new jazz.

A family picnic in the country provides a blessed respite from the big-city madness. An automobile outing to an early airfield follows. The set is complete with an old Jenny plane, madcap figures from the Roaring Twenties, and a handful of genuine vintage autos.

Finally, our vehicle passes a small procession of more automobiles heading for the open road. First comes a 1939 Cadillac with a "Just Married"

sign, weaving along the highway. The somewhat frantic bride has her head out the window. The Cadillac is trailed by a 1947 Buick convertible packed with college kids and ukeleles, a 1955 Chevy station wagon carrying an entire Little League baseball team, a 1966 Pontiac bearing the total brunt of the all-American vacation: bicycles, bedrolls, dinghies, surfboards, and a family somewhere under the debris. Flying behind each car is a blown-up version of a magazine cover of the period: *Colliers, College Humor, Vanity Fair, Free Wheeling.*

The grand finale is a "speed-tunnel" dash. Surrounded by filmed environments giving the illusion of pell-mell speed, we get to ride a snowmobile through a New England landscape, pilot a crop-dusting plane, hurtle down a steep-sloped bob-sled run, and at last we slow down in time for an all-too-brief descent through the CenterCore.

In this city of the future, the towering "buildings," constructed of wire mesh, are lit in such a way as to give them the appearance of being well-defined but ethereal structures. Chase lights, fiber optics, and liquid neon show movement vertically and horizontally and off into infinity, leaving the impression of multidimensional transportation systems all working together in harmony. The intention was to suggest the spirit of future transportation without specifically indicating the means or the time. As an impressionistic vision, Center-Core succeeds impressively. On our short trip down, we curve around it, at each moment seeing it from a different perspective.

When we "land," we're still in the future, and still moving, in a way. We are given the opportunity to "ride" in three bubble-type cars of the future, designed by General Motors and projected on a mirrored surface to give us the illusion that we are tooling along in our own twenty-first-century automobiles.

This ends the ride, a perfect transition to an exploration of the ground floor, General Motors's TransCenter. The TransCenter does more than display General Motors's ideas for the future of transportation; it breaks down the process of building its vehicles to show us, clearly and entertainingly, exactly what goes into it.

A dramatic simulation of a test in a large wind tunnel graphically demonstrates the problems of aerodynamic drag. But we are shown how the loss of energy it causes can be compensated for in the design of our cars.

A show called "The Water Engine" pits nine animated characters against each other in a lively debate on what the engine of the future will be. The coal-fired turbine, the battery/electric, the magnetic-levitation, the flywheel, the hybrid flywheel/turbine, the hybrid turbine/electric, the horse, the "water engine," and the internal combustion engine, the last in general use today —each is promoted by one of the animated characters, and as they argue the merits and drawbacks of their favorite designs, we are drawn into the debate on this important question.

For the TransCenter, General Motors built the most realistic car of the future, using the most advanced thinking from scientists around the world on what materials and techniques would be available and feasible ten or twenty years from

A 20-foot prefabricated tree—an oak to be used in the picnic scene—looks right at home in the real outdoors, where it is being painted.

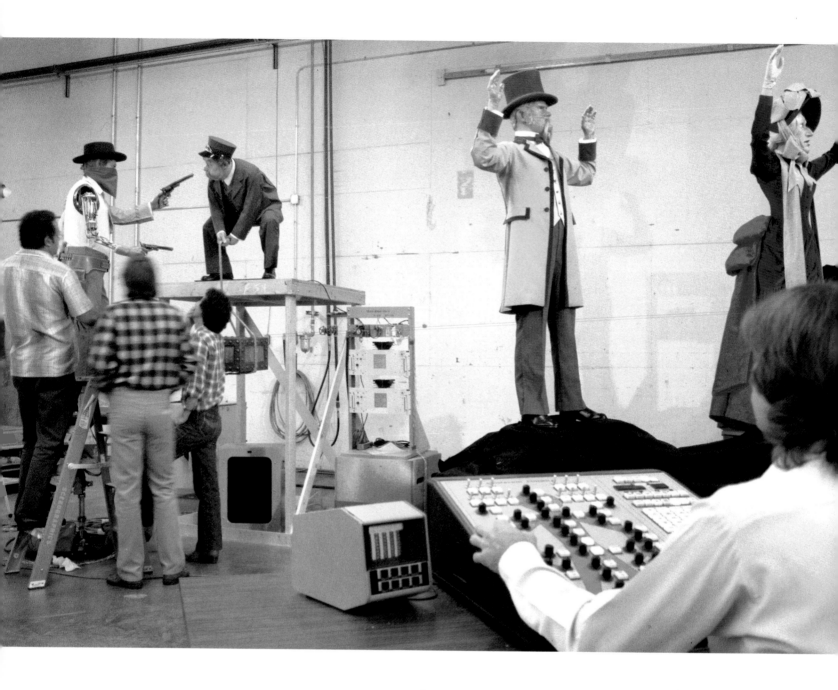

In TransCenter's show "The Bird and the Robot," the robot (named Tiger) breaks into show business under the tutelage of the Bird. Tiger performs a variety of tricks for the audience, beginning with simple things such as rolling over and playing dead, and ending with a flourish as he conducts a symphony orchestra. In this storyboard drawing at right, the robot, who up to now has been quietly working wonders in automobile factories, has learned to demand his just rewards.

now. The engineers also took into account government regulations, so that if in 1995 someone took the car out for a spin, it would be not only up to date but also legal.

In Design 2000, we can marvel at this "future car." Moreover, all the steps that went into its construction are set out for us. Beginning with studies of the needs of the public and of safety and performance factors, the designers then made several sketches of the prototype car of tomorrow. The results of different tests influenced the models that were next built. In a full-sized "seating buck" displaying an advanced electronic dashboard, the driver sees all of the gauges as ghost images in the windshield, so he never has to take his eyes off the road.

Other displays include an amusing vaudeville turn performed by "The Bird and the Robot." The Robot, which represents the new robotic technology being used in car manufacturing today, is the brightest of the breed of animated performers—the first to pick up and set down props.

Changing exhibits that incorporate new ideas as they come in from all over the world will make the Dreamers Workshop a fascinating display well worth several visits. Visitors who come on opening day will see the promise of magnetic levitation —a train without wheels; a "color room" where the colors and finishes for cars are coordinated; an interstate big-rig truck of the future; and other innovative ideas in transportation.

These Audio-Animatronics figures, left, are being programmed from a computer to take part in a scene of a train hold-up from the history of transportation show. In performance, the command is received as electrical impulses, which activate air hoses, which in turn activate the appropriate moving parts.

Journey into Imagination

Presented by Kodak

How do you house Imagination? Its architect conceived it as a symphony of volumes, forms, tonal nuances. The main theme is boldly stated by two great crystals of truncated pyramidal shape, the pyramid being a form associated with the earth and its creation. More delicate elements bring out the development, while the whole structure is orchestrated by its unusual colors.

A more intimate and playful mood prevails in the Magic Garden that serves as a courtyard in front of the pavilion. Here, shrubs are pruned into whimsical shapes: animals and apparitions and other figments of the imagination. Fanciful fountains strike a pleasing note; we may walk under a water "bridge" or ponder the mysteries of a fountain whose flow appears to be solid sheets of acrylic.

Inside the pavilion, we take a trip that mirrors the process of imagination. First, information is gathered, be it words, sounds, colors, or scientific facts. Then the information is stored and processed in the brain. Finally, the information is translated and rearranged, and emerges as a new idea or thought. The most important point made in Journey into Imagination is that this is a gift shared by everyone, a gift not to be used just on special occasions but every day.

We get off to a flying start as we speed through the universe; at least, that is what we think is happening. In our seven-passenger vehicle, we are actually moving in a large circle, with our Audio-Animatronics host Dreamfinder flying along with us in his own dream-gathering vehicle. This thirty-two-foot contraption is a wacky

The pyramid shapes of Journey into Imagination glisten
in the sunlight in this artist's rendering.

Visitors are dazzled by the fanciful interior of the pavilion, opposite page.

Our hosts through the world of
imagination, Dreamfinder and
Figment, are portrayed as the
lovable characters they are in
this artist's rendering. Dreamfinder represents the spirit of
imagination, and Figment—who
is created before our eyes from
the materials of imagination—
embodies childlike spontaneity.

A full-scale clay sculpture, right, of Dreamfinder in his full-dress costume for the "Performing Arts" scene stands in front of shelves filled with assorted small-scale models, or maquettes. This is an intermediate stage in the creation of Audio-Animatronics figures, between the maquette and the casting and assembling of the final full-sized automated figure.

In a model scaled at 1" to a foot, below, Dreamfinder pilots the improbable-looking Dream Vehicle, a contraption designed to gather material for some later creative use.

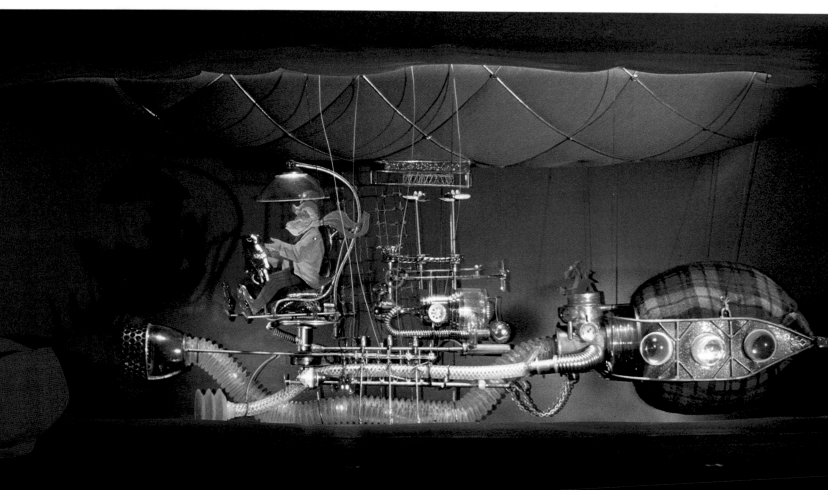

A technician adjusts the thingamajigs in the full-scale Dream Vehicle.

conglomeration of bagpipe and blimp, furnished with oars, propellers, pulleys, and dials, a Rube Goldberg type of contrivance.

Drifting past Dreamfinder's vehicle as it flies through the universe are animated "glows" representing ideas and inspirations. As our idea-gathering expedition begins, these glows are sucked up into the machine, which sends out puffs of smoke, jiggles, bangs, and bleeps as it stores the precious stuff of dreams. We are collecting these materials to take home where they will be recombined to make new things—inventions, stories, songs, pictures, all the cunning contrivances of the imagination.

Our host Dreamfinder, a professorial type who helpfully explains and interprets what happens on the ride, seems pleased to see us and welcomes us ("So glad you could come aboard"), then turns to more pressing matters.

Notes are gathered from the air; sounds, shapes, and colors are sucked in. A combination of "horns of a steer, royal purple pigment, and a dash of childish delight" conjures up Figment, a little dragon. Figment is a spontaneous creature, full of energy and childlike wonderment. He is an ever-receptive sponge, soaking up everything he sees around him. Having never been told by an adult that he is incapable of doing this or that, he thinks he can do anything—and he is not far wrong.

At sunset, Journey into Imagination is at its most brilliant, its colors vying with Florida's subtropical sky.

"Can I imagine, too?" asks Figment. Can he! A passing rainbow is vacuumed up, and is transformed into a paint set for the dragon.

Ghostly shivers, goblins, and witches are ingested, to feed the darker side of the imagination, and then, in turn, the symbols of science and mathematics—prisms and gyroscopes, numbers and letters—until at last a bell signals that the idea bag is full, at least for this excursion. However, Dreamfinder assures Figment that we'll never run out ("One new idea always leads to another") as we cruise into the Dreamport.

In a vast, busy storeroom—representing the brain—the booty of our expedition is being unloaded into appropriate containers: jars, drawers, cartons, a boiler-*cum*-washing machine called the Imaginometer.

The storeroom may strike us as being disordered—in the science area, the helium holder is floating away, and lead bursts the bottom of a metal container—but there is an appropriate place for everything. Deep thoughts, for instance, are stored in a diving bell.

Lightning bolts crackle in the nature section, while the "winter days" crate chatters with cold, and morning mist wafts from an atomizer. Sound effects are stored in a filing cabinet whose drawers pop open to emit an assortment of uncanny creaks, chirps, groans, and buzzes. Theatrical material is stored in a big trunk equipped with applauding hands; musical notes hum and twitter in an oversize birdcage.

From the Dreamport, our ride takes us into a series of spaces where the elements that were gathered and stored are recombined, each area featuring a new twist on a familiar theme—the very essence of imagination.

In the realm of "Art," Dreamfinder is painting an opalescent mural with an optic-fiber brush; farther on, a fantastically shaped, pure white forest-garden takes color under shifting, caressing lights, while mirrors reflect and distort the otherworldly mindscape.

In "Literature," Dreamfinder plays the console of a giant typewriter from whose volcanic top letters explode, then drift down as words into a book. Words like "tumble" of course tumble, and trembling words tremble, and once in a while a word like "genie" or "fairy" escapes and floats off to wherever genies and fairies go.

On one side of "Performing Arts" are the accouterments of stagecraft: we hear applause, laughter, music, and see the glare of klieg lights. On the other side are the backstage tools: costumes, scenery, makeup.

Figment is still trying on costumes as the two sides merge to perform what might be described as the dance of the laser beams, which flows from ballet to cancan, from precision high kicks to acrobatics.

We crash through the star-studded dressing room doors and, in the twinkling of an eye, the stars turn into mathematical symbols in a clever bridge to the last area, that of "Science."

In the center of a rotunda Dreamfinder stands at a console, manipulating a bank of screens designed to show how the arts of science and technology have given us the tools to explore realms we cannot see with the naked eye. Covering biology, botany, minerals, space, and man, Dreamfinder's many-splendored machine has the ability to see far (the heavens) and near (microscopic organisms), to speed up (the growing process of a plant) or slow down (the movement of human muscles).

Figment, the eternal imp, gets caught in the machinery and is stretched, compressed, slowed

Holding a pot of rainbow colors, Figment paints a fantasy landscape in the realm of "Art."

CHILDISH D...

IMAGINOMETER

Ideas and images are sorted and stored in the Imaginometer. This model is scaled at 1" to a foot.

The Dreamport storeroom holds all of the elements of
imagination, including a pigment-mixing machine, far
left, a diving bell for deep thoughts, center, and a box
of "childish delight," far right.

A technician works on the laser system to be used in the "Performing Arts" scene, while a laser image of Figment smiles overhead.

down, and speeded up, recovering just in time to star in the ride's grand finale, arrived at down a spiral of pulsating motion-picture film.

In a gentle reminder that with a little imagination we can all be what we want to be, Figment, poised in the center of a film reel, does his last little dance. Around him, filmed images of our indefatigable little guide, variously garbed as an astronaut, an athlete, an actor, a scientist, join him in synchronous song and dance.

And, in case we missed the point that the whole presentation is about *us* and our innate capabilities, the last thing we see is a framed photograph of our own party in the vehicle, taken at a point earlier in the ride.

When the show was being designed, there was some discussion as to exactly where on the ride the photograph should be taken, the point where we and our ride-mates would be most likely to make facial expressions of delight and wonderment.

They needn't have worried: it could have been anywhere.

The ride is so delightful and engaging that, when it ends, we are left with a compelling urge to create something. This reaction is spontaneous, but it is naturally provided for by the canny show planners. Immediately ahead is a magic hall called the Image Works, where we may try our hand at a wondrous array of the creative tools of the future, inspired by our Journey into Imagination.

The warm and welcoming atmosphere is designed to overcome any hesitation caused by the sight of all that electronic wizardry. And, of course, once you dive in, you'll be hooked. Just grab, for example, a "paintbrush" in one of the consoles of the Magic Palette and let fly on your individual screen. Paint anything you like, in "colors" you've never seen before. There's a pot of rainbow colors, another of Cheshire Cat tails. One "ink" gives the impression of Cubism, another of circular candy stripes. The harder you press, the thicker the line, and if you slip up, dip your brush into "erase," which will wipe it out, and start all over.

Have you ever had a secret yen to conduct an orchestra? Move over to the Electronic Philharmonic, take your place on your own private podium, and face the music. With a wave of your hand, you can control the volume of the string section, the brasses, the woodwinds, the percussion—and watch magical notes flow from the instruments.

Leaving your symphony—hopefully not unfinished—you wander about like a child in an enchanted toyshop.

Choose the elements to create a gargantuan image in a kaleidoscope: with a turn of a knob, change the pattern, pick out a swirl of color for a liquid effect.

When you press the keys of the beautiful Bubble Organ, they not only bubble, they also bring forth brightly colored spheres that you can combine and overlap and mix and meld on a screen.

Play with the deliciously prickly Pin Screens,

Trees and shrubs have been pruned into fanciful shapes in the Magic Garden, through which visitors throng to Journey into Imagination.

In this early artist's rendering of the "Image Technology" segment of the ride, Figment joins the audience watching images on giant strips of motion picture film, including a shot of the fire-spouting dragon from Walt Disney's Sleeping Beauty.

The "Image Technology" scene was translated from artists' renderings like the one opposite this model, scaled at 1" to a foot. A technician is checking it out at eye-level.

then take your turn at the Light Writer, where you, too, can create your own laser show. On one of four great plexiglass "planets," you control the swirling, spiraling laser patterns, selecting size, speed, shape.

Now on to the Sensor Maze, subtitled "It Knows You're There," which provides an artistic funhouse experience. A tunnel of neon rings assigns you a personal color, which escorts you through the giant tube to the Vibrating Mirror. Made of Mylar, the crinkling, flexible mirror, lit by a strobe, shows you coming and going in an unending pattern of zany distortions. Among other oddities of the maze is the Lumia, a voice-activated light show in a giant sphere that responds to the pitch and modulation of your voice, and Stepping Tones, where your tread triggers not only color and light effects but weird and wonderful sound effects as well: a jungle squawk

In the "Science and Technology" segment of the ride, Dreamfinder uses controls to manipulate time and space. With the help of science, he calls up images of hidden worlds on the screens.

here, a chord there, beeps or growls or spooky night wails.

The centerpiece of the Image Works is probably The Dreamfinder's School of Drama in the middle of the hall. It is divided into three "theaters," each one of which puts you and your friends on center stage in a variety of situations. Using the blue-screen technique, the apparatus projects your image onto prefilmed background settings. While you act out an appropriate scene, spectators react to your performance.

The Time Machine places you in various time warps—perhaps in a cave, threatened by ferocious prehistoric beasts, or in Elizabethan England, or in the Wild West, or on a spaceship under attack by alien creatures. Sneak Preview

One of the experiences offered to the visitor by the Image Works is *Sensor Maze,* an artistic fun house whose attractions include *Stepping Tones,* below, where the pressure of feet sets off color, light, and sound effects.

The final amazing sensation of *Sensor Maze* is the *Digital Wall,* on the following pages, which flashes colors at a touch.

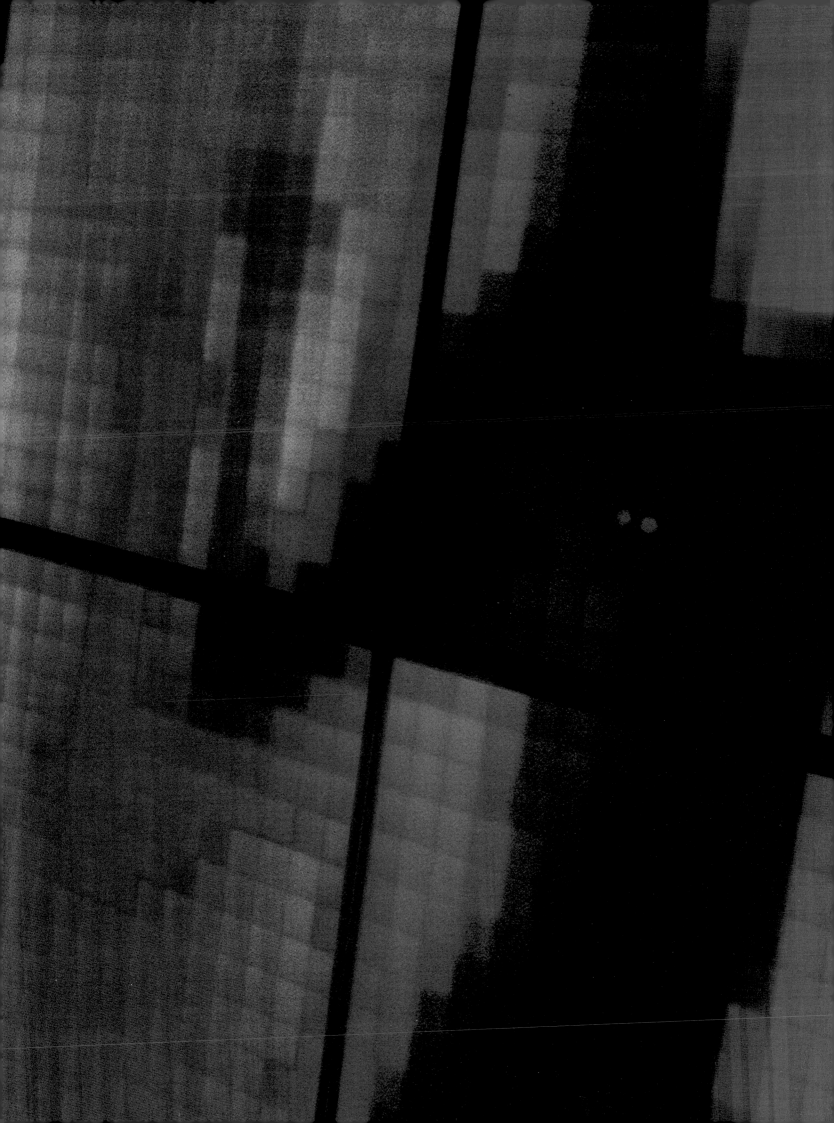

stars you in trailers for current television shows. Stunt Show superimposes your image on scenes of dire peril: on a fraying rope bridge teetering precariously between two Himalayan peaks; on the wing of a biplane about to execute an unscheduled barrel roll.

The Image Works is spectacularly successful in its goal—giving you a chance to express yourself in ways you'd never thought possible. You may become so absorbed in its myriad pleasures that, were it not for the promise of still another presentation around the corner, you would find it difficult to leave.

Besides being the largest, "Magic Journeys" is also the most spellbinding three-dimensional film ever assembled. It's about looking at the world in a fresh and exciting way, taking the images in our minds and applying them to what we see around us to create new worlds. A beautiful blend of the real and the surreal, the film also makes use of computer animation to achieve its provocative and lyrical effects.

The film begins with a group of children running through a meadow. They gaze at the clouds, which float off the screen right into the audience and then are reflected in the eye of a child.

One of the children blows on a dandelion, and the floating spores become stars, a sun. Solar flares shoot out in bursts of heat and light before metamorphosing into water. On a beach, a child flies a kite, which floats out of the screen through a window and changes into a bird, a fish, a school of fish, a flock of birds; into wings, Pegasus, a real horse, a carrousel horse. The merry-go-round rider reaches for the brass ring—and so do we, but it turns into a moon, to bats, to witches, to masks, to the Sphinx.

There are clowns on stilts, a baby's rattle floating in midair, a magician performing a hat trick—and suddenly but naturally the dandelions return as we find ourselves back in the meadow with the children. We look into a child's eye, which blinks, ending the wonderful excursion into imagination.

In "Magic Journeys," we join one of the children as he romps through the magic landscape of his imagination. In one segment, the toys in his playroom grow and grow, larger than life, then take on a life of their own—and we find ourselves in a wonderful circus. A large measure of the film's magic is due to the use of three different 3-D systems. One of them, custom-made for Disney, is designed to give pictures of a clarity and wealth of detail rarely, if ever, seen before. The 3-D system simulates human vision by using two cameras, each recording the object from a different physical plane.

The Land

Presented by Kraft

The six-acre Land pavilion embraces a boat ride, two eating areas, three separate growing areas, and an assortment of other good things.

It looks like the world's biggest greenhouse. Surmounted by a pure and pristine art form in glass, The Land is approached via a wide walkway landscaped with exotic plants and slicing through a ledge designed to resemble a cross section of the Earth.

It was an enormous site to cover, an area that kept growing, especially after it was decided that the temporary greenhouses that originally surrounded the main pavilion would be incorporated into a huge ride-through space. Now the largest of Epcot's pavilions, The Land covers six acres.

They get excited, the members of the team that put together the Land pavilion, when they talk about it. Their enthusiasm, bordering on the passionate, stems from a belief that it is the most vital, significant, entertaining, and challenging

pavilion in all of Epcot Center. The story of the land and its potential in partnership with man comes closest to the philosophy, purpose, and image of Epcot, according to the designers of the project. It's a story you can see, and touch, and feel, and even *eat!*

Allowing for their understandable bias, the elements of The Land still add up to a remarkable experience:

- A boat ride that begins with the exquisitely imaginative "Symphony of the Seed," then ventures into the various climates of the world before man, cruises through a turn-of-the-century American farm, and finally moves among actual growing areas for a mind-opening sample of agricultural techniques that are not

A cloud of balloons was released above The Land on its official opening; a gala crop scattered in the sky.

On the boat ride winding through The Land, visitors explore nature—cultivated as well as wild—with a well-informed guide.

only up-to-the-minute but that project into the future.

- A guided tour of the growing areas with detailed explanations of revolutionary methods of agriculture: hydroponics, intercropping, aquaculture.

- A surpassingly wacky, wonderful Audio-Animatronics revue called "Kitchen Kabaret," one of the liveliest entertainments in Epcot.

- A moving and thought-provoking motion picture, filmed around the globe, on "Symbiosis," demonstrating that with care it is possible for technological progress to benefit the environment.

- Not one but two eating areas: a colorful Farmers Market for fast food, and a unique revolving restaurant where one can dine in style while surveying the ride area below.

Dome to desert, French fries to fish farm, the entire complex is a harmonious integration of texture, color, and sound. To best appreciate the flavor of The Land, let us begin with the ride.

Two boats at a time, each roofed-over boat accommodating twenty passengers, move through the "Symphony of the Seed." Conceived as a reminder that all life on Earth is based on the miracle of the green plant, it features projected illusions of seeds germinating, plants growing, fluids flowing, sun caressing, flowers opening, and

As visitors "Listen to the Land," above, they will see illusions of plants growing, projected in and over a marvelous tangle of acrylic vines, leaves, and roots, in the delightful "Symphony of the Seed."

A traditional American farm, left, houses a theater where a film on modern American agriculture is presented. The boats are shown carrying visitors into the Barn Theater.

At the University of Arizona, whose Environmental Research Laboratory helped to conceive The Land's growing areas, a model of one such area is studied.

fruits ripening. This lyrical illustration of a plant's life cycle is accompanied only by the sounds of the earth and the gentle lyrics of "Listen to the Land."

The land hasn't much to say for itself at first, at least nothing encouraging, as the boat moves into three ecological communities, or biomes—rain forest, desert, and prairie—where cultivation originally was deemed difficult, if not impossible.

It really rains in the rain forest (hence the boat roofs). The perpetual fog and mist feed the plant life, so luxuriant it seems to grow before our eyes. From man's standpoint, the trouble is that the abundant table in this impenetrable jungle is set only for macaws and monkeys.

The desert, by bleak contrast, sets no table at all. Its blistering desolation is presented graphically in a setting where nothing moves but the sand—and the shifting mirage.

The prairie primeval, while not nearly so forbidding, nevertheless is rife with its own dangers. Bison and prairie dogs scatter as a lightning storm sets fire to the fields of wild grass. The fire disturbs

locusts which, flying in a dense cloud, lay waste the plain. This part of the show vividly demonstrates what untamed Mother Nature is really like, especially before man came on the scene.

Just in time, before the cloud of locusts reaches the boats, we move on to an American farm at the turn of the century. Riding through a large barn that is really a theater, we are shown a series of films that take us from early farming methods to modern agriculture in the United States—huge combines on thousand-acre spreads in the area known as the "breadbasket of the world."

The best is yet to come. The final scenes allow us to witness man turning the bounty of the rain forest to his advantage, and literally making the desert bloom. We see how, in many areas, man is actually improving on nature's bounty.

The final segment of the ride is perhaps the most exciting: a live demonstration of modern agriculture. The Land has set aside three large buildings where actual growing takes place, but no ordinary methods are used. The most innova-

The growing areas will employ advanced agricultural methods. Above is an example of intercropping. The luffa vines grow on bamboo A-frames, while soybeans and eggplants thrive below on the ground. Below, a worker lifts the polystyrene boards studded with lettuces to check the water medium—inhabited by aquatic animals—in which they are being grown, an innovative example of hydroponics.

Each of The Land's growing areas has been carefully planned. As the boats enter the Tropiculture area (at the lower part of this picture), visitors will see, on their right and left, patches of pineapple, banana trees, and cocoyams. Following the curve of the canal, the boats pass new and old varieties of sugarcane, pigeon peas, mung beans, leuceana, a large section of rice (near the top of the model), and A-frames sheltering luffa, soybeans, and eggplants. Just before the boats exit, visitors will see cabbage, kohlrabi, bush beans, pole beans and corn growing together, and Chinese cabbage, bordered by papaya trees. Visitors traveling through The Land's growing areas will be impressed with the rich variety of foodstuffs that can be produced within a small tract.

tive techniques are here put into practice, and, as soon as they become viable, new agricultural advances will be incorporated.

Space permits only a small sampling of the new agricultural applications on view. A whole day in the growing area, in fact, will barely scratch the surface. On display, for example, is a method of growing lettuce on polystyrene boards floating in a foot of water. Below swim fish who eat the lettuce roots yet do not stunt the vegetable's growth. Lettuce abhors direct sunlight, but there's a solution for that, too. Above the lettuce there are A-frames on which melons grow. The melons love sunlight, and provide shade for the lettuce.

In the Aquacell, shrimp are raised in a controlled environment. In the absence of predators, 50 to 70 percent of shrimp eggs survive to adulthood. In nature, fewer than one-fourth of one percent achieve maturity! If you like shrimp, you'll love Epcot Center's Aquacell.

In the peaceable kingdom of the Tropiculture area, sugar cane grows eighteen feet high, fast-growing leuceana trees are raised for reforestation as well as to make cattle feed, and corn and pole beans live side by side like the ideal husband and wife, each sustaining the other's needs. The beans use the corn to climb on, and repay the favor by adding the corn's favorite nutrient to the soil.

In the Desert Culture section, plants receive nutrients almost individually, through a drip-irrigation system independent of the near-barren soil. Too complicated for the average desert farmer?

New agricultural methods have enabled man to cultivate crops in hostile environments—even in outer space. This revolving drum reproduces the force of gravity, providing a down-home atmosphere for the plants growing inside.

Hardly. It's something you could install yourself, given the time and materials.

Then there are the hardy plants that grow naturally in the desert but whose potential uses have been virtually ignored until now: euphorbias, rich in hydrocarbons, can be processed into fuel to power the agriculture of the future; jojobas can replace whale oil in certain products; guayule is an excellent source of rubber. And the list is increasing.

Certain to be one of the favorite exhibitions is a sort of chain-reaction system that illustrates the marvels of hydroponics (a method of growing plants with no soil at all). By means of a conveyor rig that also affords the proper amount of sun-

light, plants rotate through a spray that provides nutrients. So that nothing is wasted, water hyacinths below collect the nutrient overflow that has dripped from the plants' roots. The hyacinths, in turn, can be processed to produce methane gas —to power the conveyor system! (Unfortunately, this last part of the cycle has had to be scrubbed —generating methane gas so close to the visitors was deemed unsafe—but the principle of an endless round, a process that feeds upon and fuels itself, will surely have broader applications.)

Following the pattern of many of Epcot Center's presentations, we've been guided from an uncertain past through an innovative present. Next we are given a glimpse of the promising future: a revolving drum that reproduces the force of gravity, thus creating an environment in which crops could be grown in outer space. A prototype constructed at the University of Arizona established the principle, but it took the engineers of Disney's own MAPO facility to perfect the model, a drum that will turn twenty-four hours a day, seven days a week. The E and P in Epcot, remember, stand for Experimental Prototype, and perhaps nowhere else in the Center is the premise more realistically demonstrated.

For us, this has been only a tantalizing five-minute ride through the growing areas, although we are welcome to join a longer, more detailed tour. If we do, we will meet, on videotape, Dr. Carl Hodges, director of the Environmental Research Laboratory of the University of Arizona. He is the consultant on the pavilion and, according to the people responsible for putting together The Land, his contribution to the project cannot be overestimated. We will see why, as he interests us in "this pretty cocoyam," makes us thrill to the story of the "wild tomato plant of the Galapagos," and reminds us that "all of human culture is based on the fact that we can feed ourselves easily and therefore we have time to do something else."

Meanwhile, we can watch agricultural experts working in the fields, and see the fruits of their labor displayed on racks alongside the ride. Anticipating that the harvest will whet the appetite, the designers planned the ride to discharge its hungry passengers at the Farmers Market.

This area was designed so that visitors could sample the bounty of the land, and a luscious visual spread has been arranged. When we first entered the pavilion on the second level, before embarking on the ground-floor ride, we could look down and see the market spread out below, a sight to inspire gasps of delight. Now at last we have a chance to explore it.

The architects have provided a feeling of boundless space, while the Farmers Market area has an authentic atmosphere of bustling activity where much is going on. Yet each market element relates to the others.

Binding it all together is the central fountain. Its colored water jets interact playfully with five huge dancing balloons, which bounce and spin in a lively *pas de cinq* on top of the sprays. Hovering near the fountain is the Good Turn, a revolving restaurant that serves more elaborate repasts; on the ground, radiating from the fountain, are dozens of umbrella-topped tables that look for all the world like the happy little mushrooms in *Fantasia*. Each table has its own lighting and soft music; there is no general glare or blare. The effect aimed for, and achieved, is intimate and casual.

In a semicircle beyond the tables are eight fast-food stalls: a sandwich shop; the Potato Store, which offers French fries or baked spuds with a choice of toppings; a barbecue counter; the Cheese Shoppe, which purveys quiches and cheese fried in pastry as well as cheeses; a soup and salad bar; an ice cream parlor; the Bakery; and the Beverage House.

It is assumed that, especially in The Land, our breakfast, lunch, or supper will include selections from each of the four basic food groups, as nutritionists recommend. Not so? For shame. High time, then, to pay a visit to "Kitchen Kabaret," where the rules of balanced diet are amusingly presented.

"Kitchen Kabaret" is a rollicking show in the best Disney tradition; it has been compared to the enormously popular Country Bear Jamboree at Walt Disney World. The show was developed because Kraft, a sponsor not without a social conscience, felt that somewhere in its vast and vital pavilion the story of nutrition should be told. So a trio of young and talented Imagineers was unleashed and encouraged to create a lively entertainment based on proper diet, of all things!

The mad and merry caper developed into a full-fledged cabaret turn with an introduction and

finale sandwiching four acts, each focusing on one of the main food groups—dairy products, fruits and vegetables, meats and proteins, grains and cereals. Try to envision a mini-version of *That's Entertainment* as performed by a stalk of broccoli, a carton of milk, a loaf of whole wheat bread, and a can of grated Parmesan, and you begin to get the idea.

The set is an enormous kitchen equipped with refrigerator, stove, and cupboards, through which a number of performers—animated foodstuffs holding small utensils—pop (not to mention snap and crackle). The star of the show is Bonnie Appetit, a "nice, wholesome housewife." In a glorious explosion of neon and steam, the dairy products kick off a parody of a nightclub show. A swaying milk-carton crooner introduces Miss Cheese, Miss Yogurt, and Miss Ice Cream ("I've got a *double* scoop for *you!*"), elaborately costumed showgirls who parade and posture in *Ziegfeld Follies* fashion.

The breads-and-cereals number, featuring the Boogie-Woogie Bakery Boy, is backed by a group suspiciously reminiscent of the Andrews Sisters

A designer works on the fruit and vegetable display in the pre-show for "Kitchen Kabaret," above. A small-scale model of the "Kitchen Kabaret" set is in the foreground.

A model of the Boogie-Woogie Bakery Boy is being painted, right, as the Colander Combo looks on.

114

but in reality composed of those stars of stage, screen, and spatula known as Rennie Rice, Connie Corn, and (are you ready?) Mairzy Oats—the Cereal Sisters!

The proteins perform an old-fashioned vaudeville routine, with Mr. Hamm delivering the straight lines and Mr. Eggz cracking wise. The Fiesta Fruit and the Colander Combo are choreographed in a zany tribute to Busby Berkeley and Carmen Miranda; it reaches a climax as Bonnie

A designer adjusts the costume for Parmesan Cheese. He and Salsa are tasty members of the Kitchen Krockpots.

Appetit descends from the ceiling provocatively perched on a glittering half-moon. The Kabaret's hit song is likely to be the rhythmic number from this segment, "Veggie-Veggie Fruit-Fruit," guaranteed to drive us happily bananas after the hundredth rendition.

It's a giant shift in mood from "Kitchen Kabaret" to the Harvest Theater, but one worth making if we are to understand our relationship with the land—a partnership on which our very survival depends. The theater's magnificent film, "Symbiosis," deals with that mutually beneficial partnership. The central theme is the delicate balance between technology's progress and envi-

An oversize stove for "Kitchen Kabaret" gets a paint job to match the small-scale model.

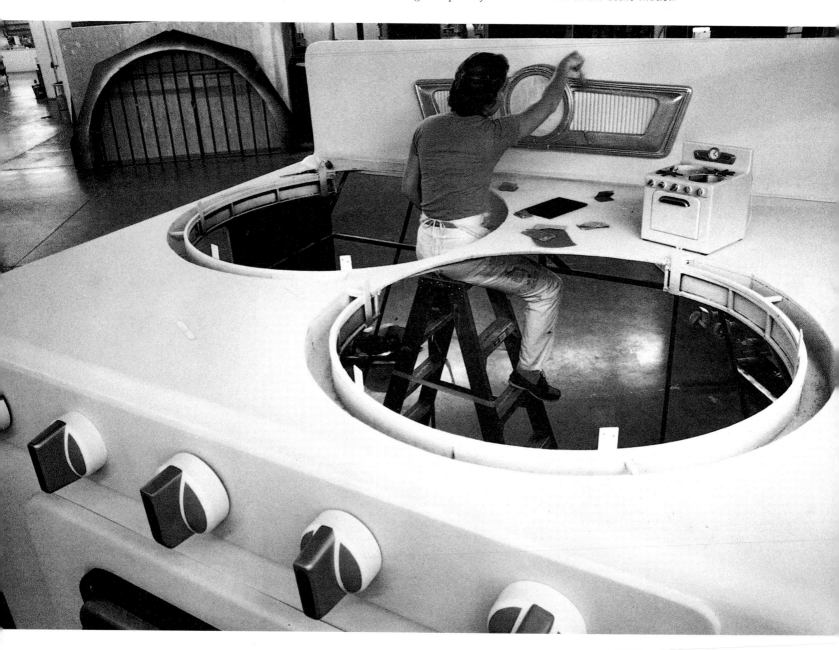

"Symbiosis," the film in The Land that shows how all things on Earth must coexist, records examples of human ingenuity improving on natural environments. In Holland the wind has been made to serve man.

ronmental integrity, reinforcing the practical applications we have seen in The Land's growing areas. To put the relationship into perspective, we are shown examples of man's use of the environment in ancient and contemporary times. Occasional scenes of technology misapplied demonstrate just how delicate the balance is.

However, the camera crews who have ranged the entire globe in search of material for the film have brought back stirring evidence of man's ingenuity in adapting his own needs to those of a bounteous but exhaustible Earth. The film's optimistic conclusion is that technological advances need not prove ruinous to the land.

"Symbiosis" is an altogether remarkable film, by turns harsh and sublime, but, above all, provocative. Which way will we go? Will we conserve or waste, restore or ruin, use or abuse?

The choice is ours.

Food for thought is one thing, but to keep the brain in shape for intelligent choices, one must sustain the body, too. An intelligent choice, at this point, might well be the Good Turn restaurant. The Good Turn hopes to serve up one day some of the very crops we have seen growing, an unusual restaurant feature. Even now, it is a restaurant quite unlike any other.

The restaurant revolves at varying speeds de-

In this scene from "Symbiosis," the ancient Inca city of Machu Picchu in the mountains of Peru is an example of how even the most hostile environments have been tamed.

pending on the time of day; people eat breakfast quickly and linger over dinner, and the restaurant tries to accommodate its patrons with a complete revolution during each meal. With its unobstructed views over the biomes of the boat-ride area, the Good Turn is able to add scenic garnishes to its dishes that even the finest chefs couldn't achieve: prairie with our prime rib; rain forest with our roast duckling; desert with our dessert.

The restaurant's decor is deliberately subdued to avoid competition with the active spectacle of passing boats below, which was designed with an eye to the view from above. There are animation effects that are tripped off by photoelectric sen-

sors reacting to the boats' progress. In the rain forest, for example, the arrival of the boats triggers the monkeys and birds into a higher level of activity. Their sounds become louder as well, so that it seems to the people in the restaurant that the boats have actually alarmed them.

As the boats approach, the rain comes down harder, and when they reach the desert the sandstorm kicks up higher, changing the color of the sun.

You will be tempted to stay at your table and take another turn around, but resist. Remember, there are only four food groups, not eight.

The Living Seas

Presented by Walt Disney Productions

One of Epcot Center's most ambitious projects is The Living Seas, the pavilion dedicated to man's relationship with the sea. This involvement is most dramatically demonstrated in an enormous seawater tank that immerses us in the watery deep. The building itself, which conveys the organic feel of a huge shell, a monstrous wave, a palisade, sets the tone for the spectacle inside.

The show begins in a cavelike area where special effects eerily trigger man's atavistic awe of the

Inside the shell-like structure of The Living Seas, above, a surprise is hidden. The early cutaway view of the pavilion, below, reveals the "underwater" tank in the center.

The artist's rendering depicts Sea Base Alpha as visitors will see it, complete with divers, marine life, and observation platform.

unknown deep with the sensation of an approaching storm. The "wall" of the grotto gradually closes behind us as the storm reaches its full fury. At length, out of a lightning bolt appears Poseidon, the Greek god of the sea, who will be the narrator for the rest of the journey to the Coral Reef.

Poseidon, who represents the power, strength, and uncertainty of the sea, calms the storm with a wave of his hand. Then he reminds us that despite man's early superstitions concerning the waters, which are imaginatively reproduced in the splendid set he inhabits, it is the oceans that make our planet unique, that indeed are the cradle of life.

Despite universal fears, our narrator continues, there were a few people with the fortitude and spirit to seek beyond; the sea god invites us to enter into that spirit—to "part the waves to understanding"—in the voyage to come. There is

In the research area of the pavilion, visitors watch divers preparing to enter the tank. Observation modules enable visitors to follow the divers' activities once they are inside the tank.

another crash of thunder, Poseidon pulls back a curtain, and we board a series of little bubble-like vehicles.

We then are guided through a stylized "Cradle of Life" in the sea sequence. Microscopic and magnified views of sea life take us on a trip along the food chain, where a giant fish with open mouth charges our bubble craft, as if to make us the final link in the chain. We pass through a giant kelp forest and down into the continental shelf with its unique life forms and abundance of mineral wealth. Poseidon underlines what these sequences illustrate: the complex interrelations of the physical and biological systems of the seas, the finite nature of the oceans' resources, and the vital need for man to work in harmony with the ocean in order to ensure the stability of its ecosystems.

Now we dive to the darkness of the ocean bottom, coming up again to an immense "coral reef" 24 feet deep, 200 feet in diameter, and containing 5.7 million gallons of seawater. We are actually in a cyclinder in the center of the tank, separated from the water by only a wall of acrylic paneling clearer than glass. However, we will not be conscious of the walls, or even of the tank. We will have the impression of being in the ocean itself. Here, we are told, man in the year 2030 is monitoring and managing areas of the ocean in the harmonious fashion that Poseidon had prescribed earlier.

The underwater setting is realistically furnished with the actual fish, rock forms, and plant life appropriate to a Caribbean locale—including live sharks! The environment, designed to look like a futuristic sea base, is an actual working environment in which man and machine coexist with the sea and its original inhabitants. All around us, we see divers carrying on their tasks, often accompanied by their coworkers, the dolphins, trained to work alongside man.

Once the ride is over, a television system en-

ables us to continue to follow the divers' activities: one camera is set in place on the sea floor, another is mounted on a robotic device following the diver, and a third, either hand-held or affixed to the diver's helmet, focuses in on the work at hand.

In four "undersea" modules, each concentrating on a particular aspect of the activity going on in the tank, we zero in on specific developments predicted for the world of the year 2030.

The first module is dedicated to undersea technology. It features a diving suit of the future, in which an artificial gill extracts the oxygen from the water, thereby affording the diver an unlimited supply of the essential element.

The second centers on below-surface communications. We are permitted to "eavesdrop" on practical and experimental operations in far-off sea bases, such as one established under the Arctic Ocean.

The third explains advances in marine sciences, including, for example, the development of a new type of warm-water kelp for food, energy—it is a good source of methane gas—and pharmaceutical uses as well as for the provision of new habitats for fish. We see how the kelp is farmed and learn that it grows twelve inches a day.

The fourth module is concerned with communication between man and the sea-dwelling mammals. Through a translating computer, dolphins can "talk" with humans. A number of the friendly creatures will be trained to participate in this remarkable phase of the show.

As in The Land, at the conclusion of our expedition through The Living Seas, we will be able to return to an "observation module" to pursue at our leisure any aspects of the show that have aroused particular interest. Among other exciting possibilities, we will be offered a guided tour of the life-support systems that maintain the base underwater—the vital underpinnings of this dramatic presentation.

CommuniCore

Technology, meet the people. People, meet technology.

Far from being forbidding, CommuniCore—short for Community Core—is an inviting group of interactive exhibits designed to take the mystery, but not the thrill, out of technology.

Like Earth Station, located nearby, CommuniCore not only welcomes guest participation, it solicits it. How can we resist the seduction of a pavilion where we may:

- Talk to a computer—and have it answer us.

- Contribute our own opinions on current issues to an ongoing poll—and actually have someone take notice.

- Check out our next travel destination as if we were scouting the place on the spot.

- Design our own concept of a Utopian community.

- Experience what it's like to pilot a space shuttle through reentry into the Earth's atmosphere.

- Control the pace and rhythm of our own downhill ski race.

Many of these adventures are ours for the choosing on opening day, and there is no telling what others will eventually be available, since CommuniCore is designed to be in constant flux. If there is one constant common to all technology, it is that technology is constantly changing. And with this expandable structure, built to accommodate ever changing exhibits, Epcot Center intends to keep up with the times.

Located at the hub of Epcot Center, in two structures that curve around Future World's main plaza, CommuniCore also serves a central function. Besides complementing the experiences offered by the other major pavilions, such as Universe of Energy, The Land, or World of Motion, it provides information pertinent to many aspects of our lives, helping us to make our own decisions. The aim of CommuniCore is to answer at least part of the question that troubles so many of us today: "How can I cope with this business of preparing for, participating in, and shaping the future?" To try to get the answers, we can spend as much or as little time in CommuniCore as we wish.

The focus of the presentations is the relevance of technological advances to our lives. The designers have taken the most prominent and convincing examples of where the future already is making itself felt. Seeing these examples in a concentrated space, we become aware of how much of what we take for granted is due, directly or indirectly, to advances in technology. We recognize that technology leads to more efficiency, even creativity, and gives us more choices, allowing us to exert better control over our lives.

The whole of Future World tells us, in effect, that the future is not something to fear, but rather is something to be desired. We can shape it the way we want it to be. Whereas some of the other pavilions try to speculate about the world fifty or a hundred years from today, CommuniCore shows us the here-and-now and the just-around-the-corner. It represents our first footsteps into the future.

Epcot Computer Central
presented by Sperry Univac

It is the computer that makes this brave new

technological world go round, and the computer is the star of Epcot Computer Central. From a glassed-in balcony, we see all the computers that run Epcot Center in action, as well as the crew of technicians who run the computers.

The functions of the computers are legion and astonishing to contemplate. Overhead screens help demonstrate the computers' long reach: they are instrumental in the precise running of shows, efficiently carrying out the orders of the computer programmers to record and play back elements of the shows, monitor the shows as they run, raise and lower curtains, operate the lights, control the sound effects—they even help in programming the Audio-Animatronics figures. In addition to their entertainment operations, they are integrally involved in fire protection, security, energy management, reservations by the millions, and control of the attractions and ride systems.

Perhaps more than in any other exhibit, the sight of these machines at work brings home to us how vital and creative a tool the computer has become, and how many possibilities for the future it has opened up.

Energy Exchange
presented by Exxon

Energy Exchange ties in directly with Universe of Energy. If you have been provoked or stimulated by the show in Universe of Energy and want to obtain more information on nuclear fusion, conservation, synthetic fuels, or any other energy-related topic, this is the place. It is organized in such a way that if you are interested in just one aspect of energy, you can immediately spot and head for the area of your interest.

Fanning out around an eye-catching central sculpture of energy in motion, which features revolving wheels and gears, are displays and demonstrations of solar and nuclear energy, coal, oil, gas, biomass, and synthetic fuels. Comprehensive information is dispensed in several small theaters equipped with audio and video capabilities and

through numerous touch-sensitive interactive television screens with even more detailed data.

Those not seeking in-depth information will be entertained by a number of devices whose performance depends on the viewer's input. In Video Bicycle, visitors pedal a stationary bike. The increasing brightness of the rider's image on a television screen shows just how much power a person can generate; soft-pedaling here won't get you across. Driving Machine, in which visitors take an automobile trip, graphically demonstrates how much the number of miles per gallon of gas varies according to speed, acceleration, use of air conditioner and/or power steering—a number of optional factors that affect a car's fuel efficiency.

It's really an electronic library, offering something for everyone.

Electronic Forum

From the assembly of the ancient Greeks to the New England town meeting, every democratic community has had its forum, a place to meet with one's peers to discuss events of the day and to plan a course of action for tomorrow. In a very real sense, Electronic Forum is as lively and democratic as Athens's agora, and infinitely more efficient.

Before stepping into the Forum theater itself, we assemble in an exhibition area where up-to-the-minute news is constantly disseminated by means of traveling light-board signs, similar to the one in New York's Times Square, and an array of other electronic and video displays. This "newsroom" brings the events of the world to us, as they are happening, in real time. And, in a very real sense, it serves as our information backdrop for the Epcot Poll, which takes place in the Future Choice theater.

Once inside the theater, the audience of 170 is directed to the touch-button console in the armrest of each seat. Here we will register our opinions on a number of broad subjects—taxes, energy, care for the aged, education—as well as timely issues in the areas of defense, welfare, and whatever else is uppermost in people's minds at polling time.

This poll is unique in giving back immediate results, which will be flashed on the large video projection screen. You will be able to compare your views with those of the audience, and the numbers will also be broken down by group. This demonstrates how a consensus is formed, the beginnings of how policy is determined from the local to the national level. The technology used is the kind that will be available in the home, perhaps very shortly. Overall, the Electronic Forum will be polling a very important segment of the population, and will reach between one and two million people a year. It is hoped that the findings may become part of the decision-making process in government, which sometimes seems so remote.

The armrest consoles offer a rare opportunity to get a number of things off your chest and into a computer, to compare your views with those of your countrymen (as well as with the opinions of foreign visitors), to make your voice heard, to stand up and be counted—while sitting in a comfortable chair.

FutureCom
presented by the Bell System

The theme of another CommuniCore exhibit is the Information Society, a display mounted by the Bell System. Here, familiar as well as brand new communications techniques used in our everyday lives, at home, at work, and on the move, are treated humorously and informatively.

The giant Fountain of Information, the display's centerpiece, is almost a show in itself. Spilling out from the structure are elements of many different information media, keeping us busy identifying rolls of newsprint, traffic lights, computer printouts, sprays of tapes, neon signs, cascades of magazines, film, books, and assorted information.

A large (30' x 20') representation of the nation-wide telecommunications network emphasizes the accessibility of information, both to and from the remotest corners of Earth. It is a spectacular fiber-optic light display of major long-distance routes, multi-colored, continually changing, and controllable. In front of the map are six color, touch-sensitive terminals.

The less technically inclined will be diverted by The Age of Information, a major attraction where large animated figures amusingly illustrate the benefits of an electronically equipped home, office, and transportation of the future.

Another exhibit enhances a familiar experience: talking on the telephone. Bell's video teleconference system lifts this everyday phenomenon to a new level. Video teleconferencing permits a meeting of minds instead of bodies, taking the place of arduous business travel, saving time and money, and increasing the productivity of the people involved.

Guided by a master of ceremonies, guests at this exhibit are seated around a table where they can participate in a teleconference, playing a game called "Where Am I?" while watching their televised images and growing accustomed to a remarkable new technique.

Two WorldKey Information Terminals provide a unique glimpse into the future of communications technology. Visitors can use them to get special two-way video guest-relations assistance.

TravelPort
presented by American Express

In TravelPort, sponsored by American Express, we may journey, via videodisc, to the destination of our choice. Window-shopping on a grand

Visitors to *Future World* find it pleasant to stroll in *Showcase Plaza* between pavilion shows. The curving arms of CommuniCore draw them inside to see its exciting displays and participate in the challenging and entertaining hands-on exhibits. The Fountain of Information, above, is one of the attractions of Bell System's FutureCom.

scale, this method enables us literally to look into future vacation possibilities and scout the territory beforehand.

In an individual module big enough to accommodate a family, a touch-sensitive screen is at our service; like a friendly genie, it is ready to call up the area of our interest, be it skiing, tropical beaches, or even archaeology. If you have a yen to go skiing, for example, you select your preferred location: the Rockies, perhaps, or the Austrian Alps, or Canada. When you narrow down your selection to a single town or resort, you see a short film of that place. All the information you need to plan a vacation—availability of rooms according to season, food facilities, travel routes, prices—is at your fingertips.

In the exhibit space, American Express personnel also provide a variety of services to guests. Agents will fill in gaps, if any, left by the computers in planning future vacations, and they will help guests with any problems that may occur on their current holiday.

Coming Attractions

A number of exhibits will not be ready for Epcot Center's opening day, but are being developed or considered and soon may add their pleasures to the already rich and varied experiences offered by CommuniCore.

Mankind's persistent quest for the perfect community becomes your quest in Road to Utopia, designed as a large gameboard. As we move along the road, we interact with the various exhibits, beginning with famous Utopian visions of the past and moving on to present-day successes in community improvement. Finally, we encounter the ongoing experiments, plans, and technological breakthroughs that are changing our hopes and expectations for the communities we will live in tomorrow.

A computer records the information we give about our own community concerns and aspirations as we examine each of the visions, and at the end of the road, we are rewarded with a personalized computer-printed certificate. This illustrated document will reflect both our special experience on the Road to Utopia and our own approach to making our community a Utopia.

HomeStyles 2000 will showcase innovations and options for the home from information systems to home design, lighting, health, nutrition, entertainment, and more. Focusing on the art of good living and the individual, HomeStyles 2000 will highlight available and coming technologies and products in each of those areas, demonstrating how new concepts in home technologies can help right now to make daily living a more comfortable and rewarding affair.

The Space exhibit will center on the space shuttle and its planned use over the next decade. The information presented about the shuttle program, exciting in itself, will be made even more vivid in exhibits that invite our participation, including one that will permit us to pilot a simulated space shuttle through reentry into Earth's atmosphere. Other displays, both visual and hands-on, will depict different aspects of the near-Earth-orbit space program, such as the Space Telescope, space industrialization, communications, and Earth resources.

Epcot Creative Center, dedicated to the inspiration and creativity of youth, will tap the wealth of imagination, excitement, and optimism about the future at the command of young people. Working in concert with schools and various youth organizations throughout the United States, national competitions will be conducted to select the most imaginative ideas of American students from primary to high schools. The winners' ideas will be showcased here.

Tron Arcade, a speculative and playful vision of games of the future, will give us the chance to interact with intelligent machines in a wide variety of gamelike activities.

The Audio Adventure Maze will test the acuity

of our sense of sound as we journey through an imaginary landscape, avoiding dangers and securing rewards with only audio cues to guide us.

In the Electronic Playground, we can enjoy the thrills of skiing or riding the rapids in a kayak without the dangers. In these games, and in another called Magic Carpet, the whole body is used: we fly through the air or speed down a slope by shifting our body weight.

These and other games will draw on advanced technologies—sensors, the interactive videodisc, robotics, and fiber optics—never before used in game applications. While being challenged and amused by these intelligent machines, we will become increasingly aware of the important role they can play as our allies, in many other areas of our lives as well as in recreation.

WORLD SHOWCASE

World Showcase, curving along the shores of the
lagoon that connects it to Future World, is a
permanent community of nations whose pavilions stand side by side in exemplary amity. Mexico, China, Germany, Italy, Japan, France, the
United Kingdom, and Canada are good neighbors
to one another and to The American Adventure,
the host pavilion located at the center of the
group. Possibly one of the reasons there is no
international disharmony is that all the foreign
countries have equal waterfront footage.

The visitor to Epcot, putting the hero of Jules
Verne's *Around the World in Eighty Days* to shame,
can take a miniaturized trip around the world in
three hours, pausing to snap a picture of the
Doge's Palace and campanile in Venice, Italy,
the Eiffel Tower in Paris, France, a garden and
Shogun's castle in Japan, and similar famous tourist sights at the other pavilions.

While The American Adventure is housed in a
single structure, a magnificent Georgian mansion,
the other pavilions have buildings, streets, gardens, and monuments that are designed to give
the visitor an authentic visual experience of each
land. In truth, after a tour of the World Showcase
countries, you feel that you have really "been
there."

A battalion of Epcot designers and architects
has re-created entire mini-towns, complete to the
last detail of the least roof, while commercial
firms from the participating nations have stocked
a broad variety of shops with enough merchandise
to satisfy the most avid shopper or browser.
Everything sold in the pavilions' shops has been
made in the countries represented.

Restaurants, meanwhile, offer the cuisines of
many lands, and a German beer garden and a
British pub provide sustenance of another kind.
Moreover, the pavilions have their own shows or
rides, giving yet another dimension to the tour.
Of particular note are the film presentations in
China, Canada, and France, while a boat ride
through the history of Mexico is one of the live-
liest and most colorful presentations in Epcot
Center.

Artisans, artists, and performers, dressed in
traditional costumes of their country, add life and
zest to the pavilions: a mariachi band strolls through
Mexico; an Italian puppet show will enthrall visitors to Italy later in the season; lumbermen from
Canada's great timber and logging areas demonstrate their skills in rip-roaring style; troubadours
from Merrie England serenade visitors on ancient
instruments, and Cockney buskers in pearl-
buttoned costumes entertain passers-by with sidewalk comedy in the United Kingdom. In France,
on the streets of Paris, crowds are amused by the
antics of white-faced mimes in the tradition of
Marcel Marceau; artists on the Left Bank paint
and sell watercolor views of their romantic city;
folk dancers from Brittany and Provence perform
in their bright regional costumes.

The entertainment in Japan is entrancingly
exotic. To music that falls strangely on Western
ears, a troupe of Japanese folk dancers moves in
serene and stately steps; a man selling rice toffee
candy from his cart dances while he snips it into
shapes resembling herons and dragons for the
delighted crowd; a flower arranger creates works
of art from a few blossoms; a parade featuring

Japanese dolls and kites enlivens the streets and squares.

In China, a great dragon animated by dancers underneath its silken body snakes its way through the pavilion, joined by the laughing crowds; a venerable Chinese calligrapher will inscribe a souvenir scroll with our names written in Chinese for a small fee while we watch. In Germany, a master woodcarver yodels while he works; alpenhorns, glockenspiels, cowbells, and the music of the Oktoberfest sound merrily throughout the pavilion.

The broadening effects of tourism work two ways. Not only are Epcot's guests introduced to the cultures, customs, crafts, and foods of other lands, but on the staff of each pavilion are about a dozen young men and women from that country, giving them a chance to meet Americans and other nationals. Through a program called World Showcase Fellowships, these youngsters from participating countries are brought to Epcot Center not only to work but to participate in an international community certain to enrich their outlook. They take part for a year in the community as employees, and also as favored guests.

During the entire year, the Disney entertainment division will focus on particular festivals of the various World Showcase countries, sometimes for a day or two, on other occasions for as long as a month. Countries not represented at World Showcase also have been invited to participate, in an effort to create a broad international ambience. In addition, once a day a Festival of Nations parade circles the perimeter of the lagoon.

But it is at night that World Showcase promises to be at its most seductive. With dramatic stage lighting illuminating the famous international landmarks, and with a concentration of fine dining facilities probably unequaled in such a small area anywhere in the world, a stroll through World Showcase will prove irresistible. A spectacular show mounted on a convoy of barges cruises the lagoon's waters, presenting filmed extravaganzas and firework displays for the people on the shores.

As the evening draws to a close, the crowds drift toward the American Adventure pavilion where dancers and musicians from all the other countries gather for a sensational international pageant in the America Gardens amphitheater. Against the backdrop of World Showcase Lagoon and the gleaming pavilions of Future World, the single large company unites in songs and dances that form a stirring finale to the day's adventures at Epcot.

In time, many more countries will choose to become a part of World Showcase—the possibilities are virtually limitless for the establishment of a true community of nations at Epcot Center.

135

The American Adventure

The centerpiece of World Showcase is The American Adventure, housed in this handsome Georgian building. From the model being painted in California, above, to the completed structure in Florida was a giant transcontinental step.

Considering Epcot Center's present layout—everything fitting so neatly and smoothly, as if it could be no other way—it is hard to imagine that in its original conception, the American Adventure pavilion was to be smack in the middle of Future World, where Showcase Plaza now stands. Moreover, it was planned as a sleek contemporary edifice, a mammoth ultramodern structure on stilts, somewhat akin to the Hirshhorn Museum in Washington, D.C.

As the host to all the guest pavilions from other countries, the American Adventure pavilion was intended as a huge walk-under facility with a ride-through attraction above, a kind of bridge between Future World and World Showcase. In theory, visitors would stroll under the pavilion toward the lagoon, from which vantage point the foreign pavilions—France, Mexico, Canada, Japan, Italy, China, and all the others —would beckon invitingly.

Our hosts in The American Adventure's dramatic trip through this country's history are Benjamin Franklin and Mark Twain, two remarkable Audio-Animatronics figures. The spirit of the characters was first suggested in these detailed and expressive paintings.

Gradually, the role of the pavilion was reexamined. For one thing, it would be an ungracious host indeed who stood aloof from his guests and refused to mingle. For another, as attractive and interesting as the World Showcase might be, Epcot Center's planners felt that it would strengthen its appeal to have an anchor on that side of the lagoon, a show magnetic enough to draw visitors. Once there, of course, visitors would find that the charm and beauty of the countries of this world would more than hold their own with the marvels of tomorrow's.

Its relocation determined, the pavilion's architecture came into question: it was immediately obvious that a contemporary structure would strike an odd note among the more traditional facades of its neighbors. With the show itself having metamorphosed into a lively history of America, a colonial-style building seemed to fit the requirements on all counts. Furthermore, in keeping with the good-host role, it would not dwarf its neighbors.

The building, at once stately and inviting, makes the visitor feel at home while conveying a sense of grandeur. The goal of the architect was to give the impression that this is America's mansion.

This, too, was the intent of the designers of the show that takes place in the mansion, and how well they succeeded! It was not an easy task, especially in view of the restrictions imposed by logistics, restrictions most notably including a running time of only twenty-nine minutes.

The theme that would structure the show—something relatively simple and, above all, workable—was the most important, and most elusive, element. The unifying theme that finally emerged is that America is ultimately a nation of pioneers, of dreamers and doers, driven by the kind of venturesome and restless spirit that feeds on challenges, revels in milestones, thrives on innovations.

The story of America in twenty-nine minutes?

Even given the legendary Disney optimism, energy, and enterprise, can a coherent history of America be presented in less than half an hour?

One could hit just the high spots, of course. But what about the low spots? There's no denying the practice of slavery and the ensuing carnage of the Civil War. There's no denying the Great Depression, the Vietnam conflict. Should one simply wave the flag, gild the lily, damn the torpedoes? Even given what must surely, and appropriately to the American Adventure, be an upbeat theme, can one ignore the tragedies of John F. Kennedy and Martin Luther King? Can pollution and crime be expunged from the collective American conscience, even for twenty-nine minutes?

Possibly. After all, we are here to be entertained, not bludgeoned with Pearl Harbor or the Valentine's Day Massacre.

Entertained, surely, say the Disney people. But informed and encouraged as well; even inspired.

Were the Pilgrims "inspired" during those first bleak and brutal years? Was the ordinary foot soldier imbued with the American Dream during his excruciating winter at Valley Forge? Were the apple sellers of the Depression convinced of a bright tomorrow?

Far more important, did the people of America learn from their common calamities, derive strength, even enlightenment, from them? Have not Americans historically hitched up their trousers, rolled up their sleeves, and pushed on to an uncertain future with a will and a verve unequaled in history? Have they not only survived but thrived?

We have, say the creators of The American Adventure, and we will continue to do so.

The negative aspects of our history are shown, then, but with one proviso: "If the event, no matter how tragic, has led to some improvement —a new burst of creativity, a better understanding of ourselves as partners in the American experience—we have included it."

And if you ask yourself why they didn't include

The wintry panorama is from an episode in The American Adventure depicting the Pilgrims' first bitter winter in the new land.

141

Sculptors work in clay on one of the Spirits of America —the Spirit of Individualism—left, as well as on Mark Twain, below, and Ben Franklin, right. The Twain and Franklin busts will be models for later Audio-Animatronics heads who move their eyes, mouth, and "skin," as if they were alive.

this, how they possibly could have ignored that, you won't be alone. The Disney people themselves have been asking the same questions for years, since they first conceived the show, subsequently reworked a thousand times. But, chances are you won't be posing the questions at the end of the show. Chances are you'll be too stunned by what you see and hear. And, yes, inspired.

For The American Adventure, given the restriction of twenty-nine minutes, is quite simply the best story of America ever told.

The decisions that the Imagineers were faced with were staggering. Inclusion of certain scenes and historical figures was, of course, mandatory: the Boston Tea Party, the victorious world wars, the moon walk; George Washington, Susan B. Anthony, Neil Armstrong.

Other choices were not so simple. How to portray the opening up of the West, the driving in of the Golden Spike, or the even sharper drive of the immigrants who pushed on to a new life? Should Betsy Ross be included? Charles Lindbergh? Marilyn Monroe? What about Al Capone?

Who, finally, should narrate the show? Ben Franklin and Mark Twain were early favorites, and indeed lasted the course, Franklin for his cheery gifts of insight and invention, Twain for his more cautious approach couched in wry humor, the perfect foil for the irrepressibly optimistic Ben. Ben and Mark hold the show together, remarkable figures who talk and gesticulate, and in Ben's case, even walk.

As we enter the theater, we are confronted

The scene on the following overleafs is of an early smoke-filled room where angry Colonists meet to air their grievances against their British rulers and the first tremors of political revolution shake the colonies.

On the inside gatefold, the vast sweep of an early Revolutionary War battle, with well-trained and -equipped British troops on the left and the raggle-taggle citizens' army ranged against them, brings to life a stirring chapter in America's history.

145

Sculptors work in clay on one of the Spirits of America—the Spirit of Individualism—left, as well as on Mark Twain, below, and Ben Franklin, right. The Twain and Franklin busts will be models for later Audio-Animatronics heads who move their eyes, mouth, and "skin," as if they were alive.

this, how they possibly could have ignored that, you won't be alone. The Disney people themselves have been asking the same questions for years, since they first conceived the show, subsequently reworked a thousand times. But, chances are you won't be posing the questions at the end of the show. Chances are you'll be too stunned by what you see and hear. And, yes, inspired.

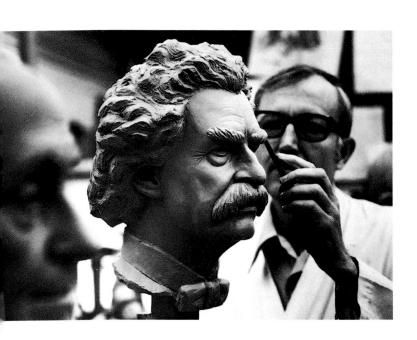

For The American Adventure, given the restriction of twenty-nine minutes, is quite simply the best story of America ever told.

The decisions that the Imagineers were faced with were staggering. Inclusion of certain scenes and historical figures was, of course, mandatory: the Boston Tea Party, the victorious world wars, the moon walk; George Washington, Susan B. Anthony, Neil Armstrong.

Other choices were not so simple. How to portray the opening up of the West, the driving in of the Golden Spike, or the even sharper drive of the immigrants who pushed on to a new life? Should Betsy Ross be included? Charles Lindbergh? Marilyn Monroe? What about Al Capone?

Who, finally, should narrate the show? Ben Franklin and Mark Twain were early favorites, and indeed lasted the course, Franklin for his cheery gifts of insight and invention, Twain for his more cautious approach couched in wry humor, the perfect foil for the irrepressibly optimistic Ben. Ben and Mark hold the show together, remarkable figures who talk and gesticulate, and in Ben's case, even walk.

As we enter the theater, we are confronted

143

The Boston Tea Party is vividly re-created in this large painting of the scene from The American Adventure. Music, voices, moving figures, and special effects bring history to life as Colonial patriots dump a British shipment of heavily taxed tea into Boston Harbor.

The war at sea was an important factor in America's victorious struggle for independence. This production painting reproduces a Revolutionary naval battle in the thick of the fighting, with American and British ships exchanging broadsides at close quarters.

with twelve life-size figures flanking the eighty-six-foot stage. These are the Spirits of America. Each realistic statue embodies an attribute of the country: a Pilgrim represents the Spirit of Freedom, a cowboy the Spirit of Individualism, a teacher the Spirit of Knowledge.

As the lights fade and the show begins, Franklin speaks first, stating not only the theme of the show but the theme of America:

"America did not exist. Four centuries of work, bloodshed, loneliness, and fear created this land. We built America and the process made us Americans. . . . A new breed, rooted in all races, stained and tinted with all colors, a seeming ethnic anarchy. Then, in a little time we became more alike than we were different, a new society, not great, but fitted by our very faults for greatness."

The words are John Steinbeck's, and the punctilious Franklin gives him full credit as the lights come up on Ben and Mark, who chat about the origins of America.

To the strains of "New World Bound," the scenes of America's beginnings come to life on a screen seventy-two feet high and twenty-eight feet wide: we see a map of the world, explorer ships of early times, the *Mayflower* on her brave and perilous Atlantic crossing, which ends with a triumphant "Land-Ho!" Then the action moves through a series of touching vignettes of that first and formidable winter faced by the Pilgrims.

It is an easy transition—far easier than it had been in real life—to scenes of Colonial days, in which disillusioned colonists are heard to rail against the indignities and injustices suffered at

This aerial construction shot reveals the massive proportions of The American Adventure's pavilion. Visitors will see its graceful red brick and white pillared facade behind which the marvels of our country's history and accomplishments will be exhibited.

The Civil War is fought again on the Disney Studio's back lot for the photographer. In the interests of accuracy, no motion pictures or photographs were made of events that took place before the camera was invented, and so the Civil War was the first subject to be treated photographically.

the hands of their oppressive British "masters."

It should be noted that the creators of The American Adventure, in harmony not only with the events of the period portrayed but also with the spirit of the time, use paintings as illustrations in the early part of the show. With the advent of the camera, photographs are employed;

still later, motion picture film is used. Needless to say, the paintings are magnificent, dramatic, thoroughly representative of the style of the era.

The Boston Tea Party leads inevitably to the Declaration of Independence. Ben Franklin climbs a flight of stairs for an eminently human chat with Thomas Jefferson, whom he finds laboring

The American frontier was pushed westward thanks to the pioneering spirit of men like this buckskin-clad explorer, who daringly opened up new territory.

over a draft of the document in a Philadelphia attic. A musical bridge appropriate to the period sounds over Jefferson's reading from the Declaration, introducing the war it inspired.

No effort is made to glorify combat, despite the nobility of its cause. At Valley Forge, in fact, a couple of cold and hungry sentries, in the eternal tradition of soldiers, grouse over their lot while, far to their rear, a mounted George Washington keeps lone and silent vigil over the future of his country.

The war won, America begins to flex its muscles, commencing the push westward on the bent but proud backs of its doughty pioneers, men and women of every origin and hue. At the same time, a few courageous black slaves hazard a more desperate journey—a journey north to freedom.

In a startlingly effective juxtaposition of halcyon rural America with harsh reality, a lone figure is seen floating on a raft down Twain's beloved

The talking heads of Ben Franklin, Will Rogers, and Mark Twain, left, are being programmed to demonstrate how these Audio-Animatronics figures will sound. Chief Joseph of the Nez Percé Indian tribe, above, appears in The American Adventure, mourning the loss of his people's lands.

Mississippi. As we float with him, we hear the sounds of the river, crickets and frogs in concert, and off somewhere, someone strumming a banjo.

The figure on the raft is Frederick Douglass, and the sounds *he* hears are "the noise of chains and the crack of the whip." Douglass escaped from slavery and became a noted abolitionist, joining his eloquent voice to the strong voices already raised against the practice of slavery. Their cause prevailed, but the country split apart on the issue.

Tension mounts as we watch a Missouri family being photographed by Mathew Brady—perhaps the family for whom the song "Two Brothers" was written. The brothers argue; a family is torn asunder. One brother joins the Union Army, the

159

other the Confederate; and in a series of Brady's remarkable Civil War photographs, the painful story unfolds.

The conflict over and the wounds bound up, the nation resumes its westward drive with vigor, renewed and revitalized by a fresh wave of immigrants, each with his own skills, his own contributions.

A euphoric time, a euphoric sequence, but again we are caught up short. In a panoramic spectacle, at the same time magnificent and ineffably sad, Chief Joseph of the Nez Percé tribe stands alone in the vastness of the prairie that once was the domain of his Indian brothers, and which he fought valiantly, but unsuccessfully, to retain. Twain speaks for the audience in remembrance of "our long, painful journey through the frontiers of human liberty."

Another group was warming to the fray, as Susan B. Anthony makes abundantly clear in the next scene. The pioneer suffragette joins the distinguished group of Dreamers and Doers honored throughout the story of America as she pursues her passionate cause in Philadelphia's Exposition Hall during the celebration of the nation's centennial.

Twain is with us again while Alexander Graham Bell and Andrew Carnegie introduce us to a Parade of Inventions marking yet another frontier: the frontier of ingenuity. Engravings of great inventions of the era (including the light bulb, the steam tractor, the vacuum cleaner, Edison's phonograph) are ingeniously animated in a sequence concluding with the flickering image of an early Wright Brothers flying machine—the show's first motion picture—signaling the wings of change overtaking America.

America is indeed changing, so fast and furiously, it seems, that someone must step in to preserve an irreplaceable component of its heritage, the land itself.

Someone does. Theodore Roosevelt meets on a mountaintop in Yosemite with naturalist John Muir to lay the foundations of the national park system.

America's concerns shifted from domestic to international affairs with the advent of World War I. This "war to end all wars" is represented by the filmed re-creation of a Spad-Fokker dogfight between Eddie Rickenbacker and a German ace over the battlefields of France. It is a striking aerial sequence, and it sets the stage for a newsreel montage of Charles Augustus Lindbergh's extraordinary solo flight across the Atlantic in 1927.

But America's path to progress is erratic, and two years after Lindy's triumph, the stock market crash plunges the country into a severe economic depression. Several bowed but unbroken characters relax on the porch of a run-down gas station-*cum*-general store, keeping their spirits up with rueful jokes about hard times. A radio is turned on, and a strong voice offers hope: it becomes evident that no nation, however despairing, could possibly have hit the depths, with no hope of recovery, and still have spawned a president with the strength of Franklin D. Roosevelt. The stage darkens, and Roosevelt appears. He appeals to the courage and determination that run through America's history ("the only thing we have to fear is fear itself"). He is followed by humorist Will Rogers, who delivers himself of some homespun wit while twirling his lariat. Sure enough, the country's fortunes slowly begin to rise.

Still recovering from the Depression, America faces up to another challenge, World War II, limned this time not through battle scenes but rather by way of a busy home-front shipyard, one of the places where the war was won. Rosie the Riveter, one of tens of thousands of women across the land to enter into the defense effort, takes a short break from patching up a war-pocked submarine to chat with a sailor on leave.

A collage of images brings us from World War II to the present. We see a vast sky, alive with vaporous colored clouds. As in a daydream, the clouds begin to assume shapes.

160

In an exciting film sequence, left, the World War I aerial dogfight between Eddie Rickenbacker in his Spad 13 and a German ace in a Fokker Triplane is reenacted.

This detailed model, below, of a rural general store was created for the sequence in The American Adventure that concerns the severe depression of the 1930s. Apples sold for a nickel apiece, gas was 18¢ a gallon, men had plenty of leisure in which to lounge around and listen to someone strumming a banjo—because they were out of work. It was not the best of times, it was not the worst of times.

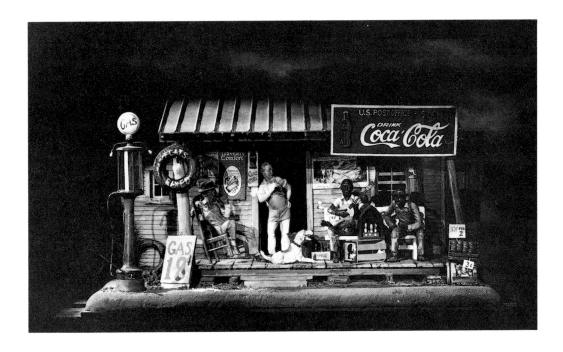

The Audio-Animatronics banjo player, right, gets his strumming hand adjusted.

The actual set, below, complete with Audio-Animatronics figures, is being programmed for words, actions, and sound effects that follow a carefully prepared script.

Twain and Franklin, on the platform beneath the torch flame of the Statue of Liberty, wind up their tour through American history with Thomas Wolfe's hopeful words about the American promise.

To the strains of "Golden Dream" the shapes take form, become pictures of memorable moments: Jackie Robinson sliding into second base; Marilyn Monroe entertaining the troops in Korea; Albert Einstein; John Kennedy addressing a crowd ("Ask not what your country can do for you . . ."); the Peace Corps; Martin Luther King ("I have a dream . . ."); Joan Baez at Woodstock. An astronaut plants the American flag on the moon. The camera moves in, pulls back, picks out a detail, sweeps across a panorama. The country's collective memory is rekindled.

Predawn New York, its fabulous skyline in silhouette, fills the screen. Then the glowing torch of the Statue of Liberty takes the stage.

On a platform ringing the torch stand Ben Franklin and Mark Twain, pondering America's past and addressing themselves to America's future, with concern and with some criticism, but also with confidence and, above all, with hope. After the show ends, the words of Thomas Wolfe, spoken by Ben Franklin, linger in the memory:

"To all people, regardless of their birth, the right to live, to work, to be themselves, and to become whatever their visions can combine to make them. This is the promise of America."

Canada

For I dipt into the future, far as human eye
    could see,
Saw the Vision of the world, and all the
    wonder that would be.

So wrote Alfred, Lord Tennyson, in *Locksley Hall,* and so say all of us after spending several hours in Future World. Our peek into the future has been spectacular, awesome, a vision of far-off wonders. Perhaps, though, it is time to come down to earth, to return to the human dimension, to refocus minds that by now are in another world.

Or, in the words of another, unsung, poet, it's "time to smell the flowers."

We have seen any number of miraculous new developments, and we have duly marveled, but it just might occur to us as we begin our stroll around the lagoon to World Showcase, leaving the future behind, that there is still no miracle to rival the rhododendron, the poppy, the dogwood blossom.

It is no coincidence that the first thing our eyes light upon if we travel up the right side of the lagoon is a superbly landscaped garden, the front yard, as it were, of the Canada pavilion. The pavilion designers consider nature to be the essence of this beautiful country.

It would have been almost unthinkable to omit from the plan a replica of the fabled limestone quarry near Victoria that Jennie Butchart transformed into a pyrotechnical floral display quite unlike any other. Although lacking the space of the original, this miniature version of Victoria Gardens does capture the look of Jennie Butchart's garden.

The brilliant burst of flowers is fringed on the right by a stand of Canada's beloved maple trees. To the left, flanking the pavilion's entrance, is a stand of conifers—cedar, fir, and a sampling of some of the 650 species of tall trees found in northwest Canada. Beyond, in a marvel of forced perspective, rises a mountain symbolic of the country's rough-hewn grandeur.

It is a quintessentially pacific vista of the natural world, rendered no less natural by the knowledge that the mountain actually houses a Circle-Vision theater, that three of the conifers aren't real trees at all, that the Epcot people have once again worked their magic.

It would have been preferable for all the trees to be real, but the problem of the mighty conifers was twofold. First, some of the trees, if allowed to grow to their full height, would eventually throw the entire perspective out of kilter. Second, the trunk of at least one of the trees had to correspond in diameter to that of the totem poles decorating the entrance area, since the largest pole was carved from just such a cedar.

In their infinite capacity for taking pains, the Epcot designers sent a crew to Eugene, Oregon, where loggers took them into the forest. There they selected one eighty-foot beauty and had it cut down. One of the craftsmen made a mold of the tree from which a perfect replica was cast. Two trees of the exact texture and color of the original were built, one forty-eight feet high, the other forty feet, and destined to remain so. A third, with a trunk three and a half feet in diameter, the same size as the totem pole, has had its growth stunted, as if by a stroke of lightning, before it could tower too high.

The relationship between the trees and the totem poles, which represent authentic examples

The Canada pavilion on a night of celebration.

Canada's Northwest Coast is the home of a uniquely artistic Indian people, whose totem poles represent their family trees. The Indian Trading Post sells many Indian artifacts and exhibits others.

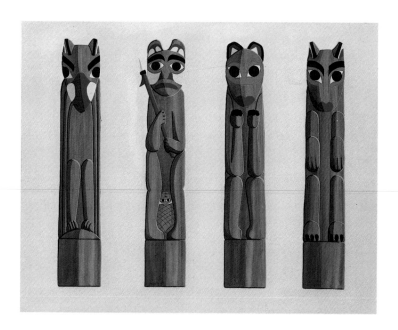

of the Indians' own unique family trees, provides a natural introduction to the Indian Trading Post, which lies inside the pavilion entrance just beyond the conifers. The Indian culture that flourished in Canada before the arrival of the white man is exhibited here. The building itself duplicates the Indians' style of adze-hewn log construction, and inside the trading post, relief paintings, masks, stone statues, and dolls may be seen (and bought).

The Indians of what is known as the Northwest Coast were the most colorful of the aboriginal Americans. They were also the most art-oriented, a unique people, isolated in an area roughly a thousand miles long, so rugged that roads were impossible and even trails were practically unknown. This incredibly beautiful land of snow-capped mountains, rock-walled fjords, and majestic glaciers might well be called the "totem pole region."

The Hôtel du Canada's French Gothic majesty rises behind the formal Victoria Gardens where visitors stroll and admire the brilliant flowers.

A CircleVision camera photographs the players of a band for the changing of the guard in front of the Parliament in Ottawa. The camera films from the center of a circle so that when the movie is shown, the 360-degree screen and digital sound will give the audience the experience of being surrounded by the band and its music.

Nearby is another trading post, Northwest Mercantile, this one representative of the frontiersmen—trappers, prospectors, loggers, and, of course, traders, both French and English—who blazed a trail northward and westward through the untamed wilderness.

Even after the English settlers outnumbered the French and the country became a member of the British Commonwealth, the French communities retained their individual character. Canada's bicultural society is dramatically represented

The CircleVision welcome in "O Canada!" includes a military salute by members of the Guard at Old Fort Henry in Kingston, Ontario, who perform with ceremonial flourish.

in the Canada pavilion by a highway of coexistence: on one side of the street is French Canada, and on the other, English.

Leaving the trading posts, we cross a stone bridge, over a stream fed by a small waterfall, to a thoroughfare straight out of the turn of the century. To the right rises a hotel, called Hotel du Canada, patterned after the Chateau Laurier in Ottawa, resembling its prototype from its limestone facade of French Gothic design to its steeply pitched green copper roofs. The structure is a nostalgic reminder of the hotels that sprang up along the route of Canada's railroads as they pushed the frontiers further into the vast territory.

The hotel will not actually accommodate overnight guests, but eventually it will house a gift shop, La Boutique des Provinces, specializing in Canadian merchandise.

Across the street from the hotel is a welcome sight in any foreign city, the Tourism Information Center, an inviting house of rugged stone modeled after a thousand others in English-speaking Canada. The interior provides one of the coziest resting places in World Showcase: a huge brick fireplace dominates the friendly old kitchen, a place to sit for a moment and relax, savoring the comfort of a home away from home.

Although buildings are important, nature remains the paramount theme of the Canada pavilion. As we leave the urban area, the road narrows until we are heading down a little canyon, and then we cross a bridge to Salmon Island.

No, no salmon there; not even the Disney wizards could arrange that! Instead, a thirty-foot waterfall cascades into a lake from which a white-water stream rushes through a gorge.

It's a bit of Paul Bunyan country, if indeed one can miniaturize a legend of such mammoth proportions, and here an appropriate show captures our fancy. Woodsmen smaller than Paul, but with no less determination, compete in the time-honored games of the great forest: log-rolling, tree-climbing, axe-throwing.

With some reluctance we move on, into a pre-show area cleverly designed as the Moosehead Mine, a long shaftlike enclosure made of rocks and shoring. It is equipped with miners' implements from the heyday of the Klondike. Through openings in the mine, we can still watch the loggers at their games, until it is time to enter the theater under the mountain to see "O Canada!" in CircleVision 360.

We've seen the Canada of another era. Now we see the modern, vital, and still-majestic Canada, probably as no tourist has ever seen it before.

From the sleek skyscrapers of the Toronto skyline to the quaint old-town neighborhoods in the city of Quebec, from chateau to cathedral, from glen to glacier, we are surrounded—quite literally—by a huge 360-degree screen displaying the splendor and scope of the largest country in the Western hemisphere.

And if it's possible for mere film to capture the heart and soul of a country, this one does it.

From the front screen, a troop of Mounties welcomes us to the show; as they ride around us, each screen comes to life in turn, the sounds of the band and the horses' hoofs following the images until each of us has the distinct and ego-gratifying impression that the entire ceremony is somehow centered on us (which, in a way, it is).

Scene upon scene draws us closer into the country: Now we are inside Montreal's magnificent Cathédral de Notre-Dame, moving up the aisle, surrounded by choirboys, as the sonorities of the great organ, captured in digital sound, delight the ear and stir the blood; now we are in the midst of thousands upon thousands of Canadian geese, taking off for parts known only to other Canadian geese; now we follow a speeding train along a river, leaving the train to soar over the snow-capped Canadian Rockies, which rival the Alps; now we are at the legendary Calgary Stampede—no, *in* it, actually in a bouncing buckboard competing in a mad race for glory, in

Another thriller in CircleVision is the famed Calgary Stampede, Canada's version of the American rodeo. This event is the hell-for-leather race between buckboards hitched to six-horse teams—and the man with the remarkable 360-degree camera is catching it all.

For those who prefer their thrills on the rocks, the film on Canada offers the white-water raft race with its scenes of the fragile craft whirling on the seething water.

the thick of the noise and whirl and fun that make the stampede the classic event of the North Country.

And finally we are outside the theater again, following the streaming crowd through Victoria Gardens south, following our noses, perhaps, to Le Cellier, the restaurant in the basement of the Hotel du Canada.

And what does one eat in a Canadian restaurant? Among other things, the delicious regional dishes brought by French settlers to old Quebec —wonderful pastries, some of them made with maple sugar and syrup, *tourtière*, a beef-and-pork pie, lake trout prepared simply, farmer's sausage, and a very special mustard-roast chicken.

French-Canadians feel right at home in Le Cellier. And even without a Canadian heritage, so will you.

France

As you enter the France pavilion, you have a last chance to walk over the Seine River in Paris on a footbridge. In fact, it's your only chance, even if you later go to Paris, because they've torn down the old footbridge that used to lead from the Louvre to the quais of the Left Bank. But not before the designers of the France pavilion took a final, lingering look.

Then they reconstructed a miniature Pont des Arts, and Epcot Center thoughtfully provided the Seine in the form of a canal off the lagoon that borders World Showcase. So if, upon crossing the span into France, you catch yourself humming a few nostalgic bars of "The Last Time I Saw Paris," it is understandable.

Once in the pavilion, however, you may wonder for a moment just exactly where you are.

Are you in Paris? Yes.

Are you in the rest of France, known collectively as the provinces? Yes again.

Epcot Center has given you a little of both. Facing away from the lagoon (or from the Seine, if you prefer), you will find Paris on the right-hand side of the tree-lined boulevard, called La Promenade, that bisects the pavilion grounds. To the left, up a little street aptly named La Petite

All the charm and romance of Paris and the French provinces are conveyed in this rendering of the France pavilion. With the Eiffel Tower as its landmark and outdoor cafés to tempt the footsore tourist, this will surely be one of the favorite stopping places in World Showcase.

Rue, are the shops—not to mention the sounds and smells—of a provincial village.

Sidewalk cafés? Of course. One overlooks the Seine, a glass-enclosed version can be found just around the corner, and up La Petite Rue, a welcome way station for weary feet serves coffee and French pastries, including, of course, croissants.

Don't linger, though. Paris is one of the great cities of the world for walking, and the World Showcase miniature version, while just as charming, is easier to cover on foot.

Follow the boulevard again, past the sixteen-foot kiosk and around to the garden area just beyond Paris. Art imitates life, and if you're reminded here of the Bois de Boulogne, a vast park bordering the city on the west, the designers planned it that way.

From the vantage point of the Bois, the scene is Paris of the Belle Époque, those years of elegance and gaiety that lasted from the end of the nineteenth century to World War I. The era was known architecturally as the "mansard period" for its sloping roofs, which even today give Paris its distinctive skyline.

Chimney pots punctuate the rooftops in true Parisian style, and looming in the distance, high above them, is that symbol of "Gay Paree," the Eiffel Tower. At least the tower *appears* to be in the distance. It is a minor miracle of perspective. Constructed to scale from the actual blueprints of Gustave Eiffel himself, complete even to its little elevators, the tower rises a mere hundred feet. So you can't ride up the Eiffel Tower unless you're seven inches tall. That won't stop you, though, from using the Eiffel Tower as a picturesque backdrop for your photographs.

Also in Paris, an old bookstore invites you to browse. Inside the shop, an iron stairway leads to a mezzanine where you half expect to encounter Monet, Renoir, and Toulouse-Lautrec leafing through old portfolios filled with art. Instead, you'll find prints and posters of their works, also appropriate to the Belle Époque.

Other stores in the area sell articles made in France: perfumes, accessories, belts, leather goods, jewelry, crystal, and even postcards.

An arcade cuts through one of the buildings and leads back to La Promenade. The arcade, incidentally, offers another experience of instant nostalgia, in iron and glass: at either end you pass through a handsome re-creation of Hector Guimard's grandest legacy, the entrances to the Métro, Paris's superlative subway.

Through the arcade, then, and up La Petite Rue in the provinces, past a cozy cluster of smaller shops reminiscent of rural France. Here a spice-and-cookware shop, there a china shop; beside the country café a functioning bakery, smelling deliciously of fresh bread and the crusty rolls you can order with your café au lait. A flower stand adds the fragrances of its wares to the spicy combination of smells in the street.

At the end of the street, back in Paris, is a tourism area, constructed to evoke the late lamented Les Halles market with its overhead ironwork. By now, this sample of France should have made you yearn for the real thing, and travel representatives in regional costumes will help you make arrangements for a trip to their country. Envisioned for a future time is an animated map of France: by pushing a button, you will be able to learn what's going on in various regions—the coasts of Normandy and Brittany, the skiing areas, the Riviera, the wine country.

Ah, the wine country! Time for a touch of the grape, perhaps, and a short stroll back to the Seine brings you inevitably to the main café. Fifty guests may sit outside, fifty more on the glassed-in terrace around the corner, and another one hundred and fifty can enjoy a Gallic lunch or a light supper in the indoor bistro, Les Chefs de France.

Light supper? In France? Many will prefer it, to be sure, but what is France without haute cuisine? Accordingly, Epcot Center is planning a formal restaurant upstairs, where it is hoping to tap the matchless talents of no fewer than three of

A Disney camera crew photographs the Seine behind Notre-Dame in Paris for the broad-screen motion picture showing the most beautiful sights in France.

France's gastronomic giants: Paul Bocuse, Gaston Lenôtre, and Roger Vergé. When this dining room opens to the public, it will offer an epicurean experience not often met with in France, and probably unequaled in Florida.

With the best will in the world, there was still not complete agreement among the Epcot team during the planning of the France pavilion. One of the first concept sketches was of the Place du Tertre, the artists' colony up near the cathedral of Sacré-Coeur. Then the Moulin Rouge and the Place Pigalle were considered, but the French advisers thought that was "tacky." (It is; but tourists still love it.)

Sacré-Coeur itself, when they tried to build it to scale, looked rather Muscovite to a lot of people, with its onion-type domes. But the Eiffel Tower is unmistakable; it is one of a kind.

Out, too, went a cancan show typical of the Folies Bergère or the Lido. However, a different kind of entertainment has been provided. Entering a building that recalls the classical facade of

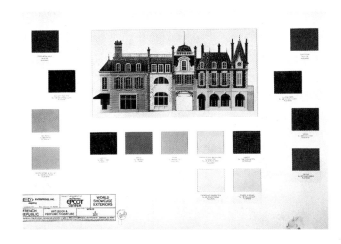

The sketch, left, for a little street of shops captures the charm of provincial France. But Paris, ah, Paris! It comes to life in the miraculous re-creation of the France pavilion, below.

The plan for the facades of France's art, book, and perfume shops, right, is carefully color-keyed to harmonize with the rest of the pavilion.

the Madeleine, you pass into an exquisite little theater similar to the one at Fontainebleau. It is actually a cinema of intimate proportions where a film on France will be shown to audiences of up to 350.

In keeping with the ambience, the movie is elegant, enchanting, evocative—and surely one of the most beautiful of all the extraordinary films shown in Epcot Center. Projected on five giant screens, each 27½ feet wide and 21 feet high,

with a total field of vision of 200 degrees, the incredible beauty of France, from Normandy in the west to the Alps in the east, and south to the Riviera, engulfs the audience. The mood is sustained through a sound track of French classical music. The result is a lyrically poetic experience, a kind of geographic *Fantasia*.

The miracle of broad-screen projection transports the audience through the chateaux of the Loire Valley; down the bustling street of a medie-

Audiences will be dazzled by the broad-screen projection of France's most picturesque and striking aspects. Among the scenes brought back by the movie crew: an unusual perspective of the Eiffel Tower, above; an afternoon in the company of hot-air balloonists, top right; and a rollicking time in an outdoor flower market, bottom right.

val town; high above the verdant countryside in the company of hot-air balloonists; into a vineyard at harvest time and among the field hands gathering the grapes; down a river by canoe; perilously close to a group of intrepid skiers negotiating harrowing precipices above Chamonix; down a steep country road at the head of a pack of bicycle racers; up to the highest gargoyle standing guard over majestic Mont-Saint-Michel; below the earth in a cool wine cellar; back to sea level on a bikini-bedecked dock at Cannes; into a cathedral; out of a walled fishing village; and finally up the Eiffel Tower from the unique viewpoint of a camera making the dizzy ascent on the *roof* of one of the elevators!

The film itself gives you a unique viewpoint on this beautiful and varied land. More than merely presenting France, it places you in it, so that you leave the theater with a knowledge of the country that others only acquire through extended travels.

And now, back to the streets of the city/village, perhaps for a last sip of wine at the sidewalk café or a final stroll along the Seine. If it's nighttime, there quite possibly will be a fireworks display over the lagoon, reminiscent of a Bastille Day celebration (the French equivalent of America's Independence Day, held on July 14). Sequenced lighting of all the buildings and streets will re-create the twinkling brilliance of the singular "City of Lights."

If the sun is still out when you're leaving, perhaps you'll see a painter down on the quai, squinting along his brush for the proper perspective.

We wish him luck. For our part, we've got our own perspective on France, and a pretty picture it is at that.

The artist's rendering of a projected tourist information center, above right, evokes the old central marketplace of Paris, Les Halles, with its open system of girders and skylight.

Au Petit Café, right, is the quintessential Parisian sidewalk café. Linger for refreshment outdoors, but don't miss dining at Les Chefs de France. Paul Bocuse, Roger Vergé, and Gaston Lenôtre, three of France's culinary stars, left, have created special dishes to be served there.

Germany

Stand in the *platz*, or plaza, of the Germany pavilion. Let its *gemütlich* atmosphere wash over you. Then, choosing your favorite angle, take a photograph, being careful not to include any of the strolling tourists. When the picture is developed, casually show it to a friend who has traveled in Germany.

The friend will probably recognize the site immediately. "Sure I know where that is. It's in Bavaria . . . No, it's near the Rhine . . . Well, I just can't place it precisely, but I *know* I've been there."

This is the feeling the designers have managed to convey in their re-creation of a typical German town. Of course, there is no such German town, nor was there ever one. Architecturally, the designers have borrowed a bit from each of their own favorite cities and villages.

Here a creative arts bookshop modeled after the Kaufhaus, a merchants' hall in Freiburg; there a facade for the tourism building inspired by the fifteenth-century burghers' houses in Frankfurt's Römerberg Platz. The exterior of the beer garden hints strongly of one in the walled town of Rothenburg ob der Tauber; the romantic castle that backs the entire setting is modeled mainly on the Eltz Castle, whose medieval fortifications tower above the Mosel River.

The secret of World Showcase's charm is: "Never take anything just as it is; search for elements and details you can adapt."

If the cityscape appears to the armchair architect to be a mishmash of styles, obviously he has never been to Germany. The Epcot designers have indeed incorporated elements of structures from the thirteenth through the seventeenth centuries, but those elements exist side by side in the most picturesque German towns, whose histories span hundreds of years. The overall effect is one of charm, warmth, solidity, and the timelessness one associates with an old and beloved fairy tale.

Yes, we think of fairy tales when we daydream about Germany, and of craftsmanship, of the romance of the river castles, of oompah bands, and of sauerkraut and beer. And they're all here in the Germany pavilion of Epcot Center's World Showcase.

We stroll over cobblestones to the center of the town *platz* with its statue of St. George slaying the dragon, a favorite German theme. This one was modeled after the one in Rothenburg.

A number of craft shops, quaint in concept, appealing in content, front the *platz*. One shop displays and sells clocks and other mechanical crafts, including handmade music boxes. Another offers a variety of German wines that visitors may taste before making a selection.

In Glaz und Porzellan, the Goebel-Hummel ceramic shop, a demonstration area has been set apart where visitors can see artists painting the exquisite figurines, and, of course, there will be a selection of Hummels for sale.

In Porzellanhaus, a store with octagonal vaulted ceilings, there are displays of porcelain wares, including place settings and other utilitarian merchandise as well as fantastic figures of birds and animals.

But the family favorite is sure to be the toyshop, Der Teddybär. Its carved wood interior sets off displays of train models, dolls, miniature castles, and a menagerie of the world-renowned stuffed animals by Steiff.

The designers' pièce de résistance is the creative arts bookshop, Der Bucherwurm, a two-story

The picturesque architecture of an old German city surrounds the cobbled Platz of the Germany pavilion.

In the Goebel-Hummel porcelain shop, visitors can watch the world-famous wares being crafted and can even buy a figurine to take home.

In the studio at WED, a sculptor puts the finishing touches on St. George and the Dragon for Germany's platz. Note that the small model in the background and the completed statue differ in pose from the version in the artist's earlier painting, opposite, which is pictured in front of the clock tower.

building with an arcade framed by window boxes overflowing with flowers. Modeled after the Freiburg Kaufhaus, it is authentic even to the statues of the Hapsburg emperors gracing the south facade.

The task of sculpting the Hapsburgs was not easy, as the architectural photographs sent to WED were shot from below, distorting the statues. A photographer in Freiburg was commissioned, and he hired a cherry picker to raise him

and his camera to the level of the statues for a series of closeup side, front, and three-quarter shots. Now, even a Freiburger might be fooled by the sculptures—except that there are only three emperors in Florida and four in Freiburg. Emperor Maximilian was left out. Political considerations? An Epcot gaffe? Not at all. All the buildings were scaled down to reduce them to more comfortable proportions. With the best of intentions, the designers were forced to drop one of the Hapsburg emperors.

To the rear of the *platz* are three major elements of the Germany pavilion, two of which, alas, have not been made ready for Epcot Center's opening day. Never mind. The third element will surely carry the day—not to mention the night, and even the foreseeable future.

The tourism area, when it is completed, will convey the feeling of a medieval town hall with suits of armor, coats of arms of Germany's states and cities, and other appropriate and well-researched appointments. There will be a visual display to whet the viewers' appetites for the real Germany, and facilities for making travel arrangements to fulfill their wanderlust.

The future River Ride promises to be as enjoyable as it is informative. An early concept has visitors boarding a "cruise boat" for a simulated ride down the Rhine and other rivers, the trip affording a visual impression in miniature of the cultural heritage of Germany's past and the highlights of its present. Among the detailed models envisioned are scenes in the Black Forest, the Oktoberfest, Heidelberg, the industrial Ruhr Valley . . . the possibilities are limited only by the planners' imaginations.

What is in place, though, and larger than life, is the Biergarten, to most tourists an essential part of their visit to Germany. And what a beer garden!

Three stories high, with tables placed around a tiered semicircle, the indoor garden miraculously conveys the feeling of an outdoor courtyard. In one corner is a tree, in another a full-sized, functioning waterwheel.

On the opposite side of the garden is a meticulous re-creation of the best of sixteenth-century Rothenburg, complete with its residences. In the center of the town square is a stage where live entertainers, including that inevitable and beloved oompah band, dance and sing and make German music.

Served with the best German beers are such traditional tidbits as bratwurst, sauerkraut, potato dumplings, hot pretzels, sauerbraten, smoked pork in aspic, sausage . . . everything that is Teutonic and tasty.

The setting is simply splendid, the sort of place we would all love to visit, and many will be loath to leave the jollity of the Biergarten. But leave we must, back to the *platz* for a last look around, while the glockenspielers halfway up the clock tower chime the hour and the band thumps out a final chorus of a rollicking polka.

Perhaps the lights are coming on now, illuminating the windows and louvers, the edge of a chimney, the rustic wooden balconies and beams of this charming town, and making it such a place of enchantment that it is even harder to depart. Maybe we can leave a little trail of breadcrumbs— or pretzel crumbs—as Hansel and Gretel did, to ensure our return.

At dusk, the torii, Japan's ceremonial gate of honor, is silhouetted against the Florida sky.

Among design details specially executed for the pavilion are hangings with stylized chrysanthemum motifs, above right.

Japan

Ah, Japan! The very name is evocative—lately of cars, computers, and televisions, as well as of cultured pearls, but beyond that, it is evocative of the exotic East, of an ancient land and its people.

Underlying modern Japan's high-tech hustle and bustle are its enduring traditions, characterized by grace, refinement, serenity, formality, taste, proportion, decorum, delicacy. And to a remarkable degree, these, too, are the qualities reflected in Epcot Center's Japan. It would be wise, then, to bow to another honored Japanese custom: bring a camera and plenty of film.

The approach to Japan is dramatic. In the lagoon is a replica of the ancient Itsukushima Shrine on an island in the Inland Sea, and in the water beyond the shore stands a vermilion *torii*, a gate of honor resembling a Japanese calligraphic

The great vermilion torii, *above, signifies good luck as it welcomes visitors to the Japan pavilion.*

In the interior of a teppanyaki dining room, below, delicious ingredients are prepared at the table.

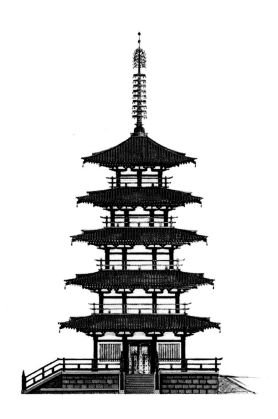

At right is a rendering of the 83-foot-tall pagoda, its sorin with nine rings and a water flame clearly outlined at its tip.

character. The *torii* is found throughout Japan at the entrance to ancient shrines.

Facing the pavilion grounds, one sees a sight to stir the imagination. Flanking the entrance to the left is the graceful *goju-no-to,* or five-story pagoda, whose stages, in ascending order, represent the elements from which Buddhists believe all things in the universe are created: earth, water, fire, wind, and sky. Inspired by the exquisite eighth-century pagoda of Horyuji temple in Nara, it stands eighty-three feet high. The roof is surmounted by a *sorin,* a spire composed of nine rings, each with its own wind chimes, and topped by a water flame, and, since this is Florida and not Japan, a lightning rod—a prudent concession to the elements of fire and sky.

The earliest model of the pagoda was based on photographs of popular pagodas in Japan. Fortunately, WED's Japanese advisers saw it and explained that these were built in the Chinese rather than the Japanese style. The pagoda originated in China, and the Japanese adapted it to their own sensibility—that is, they used less color and less curvature of the roof and eliminated much of the ornamentation, emphasizing, above all, simple lines and purity of form. The pavilion designers rectified their mistake, and their pagoda is now impeccably Japanese.

Walking clockwise around the square, we enter a formal garden conceived as an oasis of serenity. A meandering stream tumbles over a waterfall and flows under several rustic footbridges to end in a *koi*-fish pond. Along the way it rambles past formal arrangements of flowers, rocks, lanterns, paths, and pebbles that appeal not only to the eyes but to all the senses—save, perhaps, that of taste.

This last has not been overlooked by a country whose cuisine has attracted more and more chopstick gourmets. At the top of the gently sloping garden, not far from the waterfall, stands a teahouse, a small version of part of the Katsura imperial villa in the Kyoto gardens, which serves here as a restaurant offering Japanese snacks. It is an exquisite and elegant little building appropriate to the delicacy of the food it purveys. The teahouse will serve beef bowls, *yakitori* (bits of meat or fish on a bamboo skewer), and, of course, little cups of tea, which may be taken at leisure on the outside patio. Lanterns, umbrellas, and kimono-clad waitresses create an ambience of old Japan, making the site one of the most tranquil of all Epcot Center's eating areas.

Refreshed, we continue down into the court-

The Japan pavilion's skeleton, above, while taking shape in Florida, had a remarkable elegance foretelling the beauty of the finished buildings. Now the goju-no-to, or five-story pagoda at right, is illuminated at night like some gorgeous Japanese lantern.

yard and through the "entry castle"—a necessary architectural transition but a splendid structure in its own right—then cross a moat into the main castle. It is an edifice of immense delicacy, a contradiction in terms anywhere but Japan. Modeled after the Shirasagijō, or White Egret Castle, overlooking the city of Himeji, it is representative of the fortresses that in the warlike feudal period guarded Japan's precious ports and waterways. These were often built on man-made mountains, the natural variety being in short supply, and were self-sustaining environments where the ruler and his men could live for years, if need be.

Atop the fortification is a replica of the king's quarters, which will be the pavilion's VIP lounge. In the lobby and gallery, carrying out the theme of an ancient castle, are various displays of kimonos, pottery, Bunraku dolls copied from the traditional wooden puppets, as well as samurai swords,

armor, and similar accouterments of the old Japanese warlords. In time—October of 1983 is the target date—this castle will also house the pavilion's principal show, and what a show it will be!

Meanwhile, we can explore the Shishinden, or Hall of Ceremonies, originally part of the Gosho Imperial Palace complex in Kyoto, and the last stop on our trip around the square. No emperor is in residence here, though there is a king's ransom of Japanese merchandise for sale on the ground floor, and a princely feast waiting in the restaurant above.

Sponsored by Mitsukoshi, Tokyo's largest and most prestigious department store, the sizable shop offers toys, prints, incense, tea sets and accessories, a wealth of traditional bamboo products, ceramics, kimonos, kites, dolls, lanterns—every tempting product of Japan.

On the second floor, a semiformal restaurant is

"Meet the World" will trace Japan's history and legends from prehistoric times to today in a lively and entrancing presentation. These are sketches and renderings for several scenes, including the magical crane, right, who takes two children, far right, on a journey through time. Two comic characters, right center, introduce later developments in Japan by using sliding screens that open and shut on each new scene.

Several scenes from "Meet the World," top to bottom: the Japanese islands emerge from the sea after millions of years of geological upheavals. On a beach in modern Japan, the crane comes to take the children on a journey through Japan's past. Fishing was a major activity of the islanders in the prehistoric Jomon period. By the time of the Yayoi period, wet rice culture had been developed, a big step forward in the growth of inland communities. A unified Japan sends ships to China in the seventh century, and Japanese emissaries, opposite, present gifts to Chinese officials in the capital before returning home with a host of new impressions and ideas.

divided into lounge, tempura bar, and five tep-panyaki rooms where savory ingredients are pre-pared right at the table. Each area affords an unparalleled view of garden, castles, and pagoda.

Japan pavilion's show, when it is ready, will afford an unparalleled overview of Japanese his-tory. Entitled "Meet the World," it will also be the feature attraction of Tokyo Disneyland, scheduled to open in 1983. The Florida version will be substantially the same as the Tokyo show, although there will be a few changes, if only in phraseology.

Nevertheless, audiences in Tokyo and Florida alike will be fascinated by the Disney way of showing them history in a manner they've never before experienced. It's a manner *nobody* has experienced, combining as it does Audio-Anima-tronics figures, live-action film, *and* animated film.

Inside the castle, the audience is seated in a rotating carrousel theater, which will revolve in front of four stages, each presenting a chapter of the story of Japan.

The first chapter traces the volcanic origin of the islands. Then, in the company of two Japan-ese children and an animated magical crane (symbol of good health and long life), we explore the early history of the inhabitants of the islands.

Stage II deals with Japan's first emissaries to a foreign country—a splendid scene in Imperial China. Much of China's culture was absorbed and subsequently adapted to distinctive Japanese forms. A new foreign influence arrives with the epochal visit from Portuguese traders, who intro-duce the Japanese to firearms. This chapter ends with the closing of the country to almost all foreign visitors.

In Stage III, Japan, in self-imposed isolation,

develops artistically and intellectually. Here we are introduced to Yaji and Kita, guards in the family of a powerful Shogun in the Edo period, whose story is a Japanese classic. But in the Disney version they are a couple of amusing characters. Enter Commodore Perry and his great Black Ships. His visit gives rise to heated debate between Japan's isolationists and expansionists.

The scene ends with the cataclysmic expansionism of the 1940s, but Stage IV demonstrates, amply and ably, the rehabilitation, stabilization, and outreach of a modern, caring people, at once sophisticated and traditional, whose influence now extends far beyond the shores of their islands.

The show ends with the children and the crane waving farewell from the gondola of a balloon. But we can return to Japan, at least for a moment, after we leave the theater: it is there all around us, and our appreciation will be heightened after what we have just seen.

"Meet the World" continues with the Great Buddha at Nara, left, representing another influence from the Chinese mainland. The next several hundred years were a time of great internal development, during which foreign influences of the previous era were assimilated. The creative ferment is reflected in the artwork of the period, including a scene from the twelfth-century scrolls of the Tale of Genji, below left. After a long period of isolation, Japan opened its doors to Commodore Perry and now, more than a century later, the torii below welcomes visitors to its pavilion at Epcot Center.

Italy

The heart of every Italian village, and of many big-city neighborhoods as well, is the piazza. It is like an outdoor room, with space for strolling, for people-watching, and for sitting at sidewalk tables over an espresso or an aperitif. Not surprisingly, the designers of Italy decided that the centerpiece of this pavilion would be the quintessential Italian piazza.

The first thing you notice is the color. This pavilion is the color of Italy—unduplicated anywhere in the world, not even in Mediterranean Spain or Greece—a warm umber with tones of yellow and red. Add to this the good Italian smells coming from the kitchen of Alfredo's restaurant on the piazza, and the essence of Italy instantly surrounds you.

From the vantage point of a little island, surrounded by a canal cut from the lagoon to give the feel of Venice (and outfitted with several gondolas moored to those familiar "barber poles"), you get an excellent view of the entire pavilion. Dominating the scene to the left are replicas of Venice's fourteenth-century Doge's Palace and, next to it, the thousand-year-old campanile, or bell tower, scaled down but still one hundred feet high. And what attention to detail has been lavished on the palace, for many centuries one of the architectural gems of the Queen of the Adriatic!

For example, in an early sketch of the carved angels, each was holding up a cornucopia. One of the sculptors sensed that something wasn't quite right, but the originals had deteriorated with age and were difficult to make out. A burning torch seemed a more likely appendage, since flames were the symbol of Christianity. Now the angels carry flaming torches.

Another error caught in time concerned the statue of a doge wearing a single hat. Research indicated that a doge was never to go bareheaded, and when he removed one hat, there was always a little cap underneath.

There is a wealth of detail in all the buildings that perhaps only a doge or a Venetian angel could fully appreciate. Taken as a whole, it contributes immensely to the pavilion's air of authenticity—even if there are no pigeons in Epcot's version of St. Mark's Square. But the products sold on the ground floor of the palace are completely authentic Venetian imports—Venetian glass, crystal, and jewelry.

From the palace you might go next door to sip an espresso or a Campari on the open terrace of Alfredo's. This version of the renowned *ristorante* in Rome is designed in the Florentine style, both outside and inside. Truly an elegant place, it has borrowed the rich colors of Renaissance fabrics and carpeting. The only reminders of the restaurant's prototype are the lobby, its walls covered with photographs of the famous, and the kitchen, its chefs faithfully reproducing the cuisine that originally drew celebrities to Alfredo's, where their pasta was served with golden forks.

But here the restaurant walls vie with the pasta for the attention of the guests. No ordinary walls, these are based on Veronese's remarkable perspective paintings. The trick is called *trompe*

The Italy pavilion's waterfront is a replica of Venice, startlingly like the actual city, with the Doge's Palace and campanile waiting to be photographed by Epcot Center's tourists.

Venice is authentic, from the grotesque head carved on the Doge's Palace, below, to the "barber pole" moorings for gondolas. Except that Chinese rooftops would not be seen across a real Venetian lagoon!

l'oeil, and it fools the eye indeed. One wall features court musicians who look so real that you'll strain to hear their music. The east wall depicts a view from a terrace overlooking a Florentine landscape, while at the south end, the wall is punctuated by three doors through which restaurant staff comes and goes. It is only when you become aware that Alfredo's waiters pass through just the center door that you realize the rest of the crew are painted figures.

Leaving Alfredo's, well satisfied but a little perplexed by the painted tricks, you stroll around the far end of the piazza, past garden walls behind which a stand of stone Roman pines seems to whisper ancient tales of Romulus and Remus.

Next, you come to the fountain, without which a piazza simply isn't a piazza. And this one isn't just a small model. Watching over your three coins and his own retinue of water-spouting dolphins is the heroic figure of the sea god, sculpted in the style of Bernini, and surely modeled after the great Neptune himself.

On the colorful raised platform in the center of the piazza, meanwhile, there's probably some form of entertainment going on. You might stop and take a seat to watch folk dancing, or a performance of *commedia dell'arte*, the improvisatory theater born in the Middle Ages, or a puppet show. *Commedia dell'arte* was the ancestor of the Renaissance Punch and Judy show, which also originated in Italy.

Then, completing the circuit, you might pause for a little impulse shopping, choosing among the leather goods, basketry, and ceramics at the pavilion's Northern Italy building. This structure, reminiscent of a typical market-square city hall of the fifteenth or sixteenth century (and modeled perhaps most closely on a similar building in Bergamo), is, in some ways, the most engaging in the Italy pavilion. Its designers have included the small incongruities and oddities that give an old building a history, adding to its charm. Few

The great Neptune will undoubtedly cut an impressive figure as the centerpiece of Italy's magnificent fountain.

buildings remain perfectly preserved as they were when new. Over the centuries, landlords change; one year they are prosperous, and they build on additions. The next year they're a little short of funds, so they tear down part of the structure and sell the stones.

In a sense, the Italy pavilion itself is a victim of this cycle of fortune; the area which was to represent Southern Italy—not to mention a splendid replica of Roman ruins—may not be completed until 1983.

Meanwhile, the pavilion as it now stands will amply reward you with its colors, its gaiety, its genuine flavor of Italy.

China

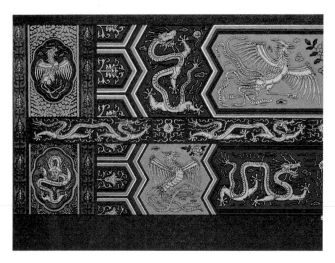

These graceful stylized dragons—unmistakably Chinese—are part of the decorative scheme designed for the pagoda's exterior beams.

As you pass through the ceremonial gate of China, you will see ahead of you an exquisite structure styled after the Temple of Heaven in Peking, the focal point of the pavilion grounds. Before you reach it, let the atmosphere of this ancient country transpose your frame of mind to a different dimension.

As a first step, contemplate the three imposing rocks by the entrance to China, each about fifteen feet high. Centuries ago, the Chinese learned that contemplation of the shape and texture of particularly lovely rock forms contributes to the serenity of one's nature. Ancient rulers, in fact, would spend fortunes to find and transport particularly well-formed rocks to their palace gardens. Sometimes they sent hundreds of men on an expedition that might last three years, just to bring back one rock of a particular configuration.

Republic of China

Concept Design

13, 1981

This early rendering gives an idea of what China will look like to visitors arriving by boat.

The lotus pool is another inducement to serenity. After gazing at the floating waterlilies and tiny waterfall, cross the graceful bridge over the pool and enter the three-tiered round temple. This structure, with its precise and delicate geometrical relationships, will complete the mental process by which you will be transported to China. The designers have put no display inside, allowing the peaceful atmosphere to work its charm without any distractions.

Your next stop is a pre-show area where a display of photographs is planned. Through the windows, you also will get a tantalizing invitation to visit an adjacent art gallery. But now you are ushered into the theater to view a remarkable film on China. Almost as remarkable as the film is the story of how it was made—a story involving delicate diplomacy, physical hardship, and plenty of drama.

The first hurdle was to get permission from the Chinese to film in their country. On being approached, they were interested but wary. Where did the Disney crew want to film? Who would supervise the film and its production? In what

The CircleVision film for the China pavilion includes these fabulous scenes of the Great Wall, above, and of children skating on the frozen Songhua River in Harbin, right.

The film crew mounts a camera rig to capture the Forbidden City for visitors to China in Epcot Center.

light would the country be portrayed? They insisted that any filming would have to be done under the strictest supervision, and declared that certain areas where the Disney crew wanted to film, such as aerial shots of the Great Wall and Tibet, were out of bounds.

After a series of talks, a group from Epcot flew out to the People's Republic of China. They concluded a visit to Peking with a special screening of *Fantasia*. The trip and the film broke the ice, and an arrangement acceptable to both parties was arrived at.

The Epcot people agreed to work through the China Film Co-Production Company, an arm of the Ministry of Culture set up to deal with foreign groups coming to China to film. Under the

ground rules, Chinese labor and production crews were to work with the Disney crew.

The Chinese would go up in the helicopters and photograph scenes in areas considered strategically sensitive. The American crew would study the videotapes and either approve on the spot or send the Chinese aloft again. If any problems arose, it was hoped that they might be circumvented as the crews got to know each other.

The film crew scouted for two months, then began shooting in the summer and autumn of 1981. To capture the contrast of the seasons, they returned in winter, and ended filming in the spring of 1982. Their mission was a relatively straightforward one: to bring back a CircleVision film that would rival anything done before. Since

The Disney filmmakers were the first foreigners allowed to shoot Tibet's capital, Lhasa, known as the Forbidden City. The magnificent Potala Palace, left, once the seat of the Dalai Lamas and the spiritual and temporal center of traditional Tibet, occupies an entire hill overlooking the city.

The army of life-size terra-cotta warriors and horses, right, who have stood guard in the Mausoleum of the first Emperor of Qin, Shi Huang, for 2,200 years figure in the amazing film on China.

the CircleVision film was to be the keystone of the China pavilion, their success was crucial.

The first film was flown back to the United States in September of 1981. A handful of WED executives, project coordinators, and film technicians perched nervously on metal folding chairs in front of a series of giant screens in a huge sound stage at the Walt Disney Studios in Burbank. The film had not yet been edited. There was no sound track.

Materializing first on the center screen, then expanding beyond peripheral vision, was a panorama of the ineffable vastness of Mongolia. The image mesmerized the small audience. No one spoke.

On a corner of one of the screens, a horseman appeared. Then another, and another. Soon half a dozen Mongolian tribesmen were galloping full tilt across an endless rolling plain, their movements so smooth, so natural that their mounts seemed to be on casters.

The camera zoomed in on their faces—timeless, stern, striking—as the horsemen charged over the rise of a hill. Then, as the horses were slowed to a canter, the hard, chiseled faces began to relax. One of the riders turned and smiled at a companion, whose reciprocating grin would have disarmed Genghis Khan.

Half a world away, the smiles were picked up and reflected on the faces of the viewers. A ripple of applause echoed off the walls of the cavernous room.

The China pavilion was in business.

The film will show all the classic sights long hidden from Western eyes: the Great Wall, the Forbidden City, the Summer Palace, the Yangtze River, the Leshan Buddha near Chengdu in Sichuan Province, and the excavation of the Qin Shi Huang Tomb, where row upon row of life-size clay warriors and horses have stood guard for centuries.

With luck, the Disney crew will also get some superb, unique shots of Anhui Province. There's one vantage point they could not reach by helicopter; it's a strategic area. So to reach it the crew had to carry a three-hundred-pound camera up the 16,700 stone steps carved into Huangshan Mountain, one of the five sacred mountains of

ancient China. The Chinese members of the crew are rugged, but even they began to worry when the Americans said they were going to Tibet.

Although the film has elements of a travelogue, it is a great deal more than that. An ancient poet, Li Po, steps out of his time to guide the audience through China's history, culture, and spectacular spaces. In instances when artistic detail would be lost on a large wraparound screen, paneled screens are employed.

Yet the very sight of the immensity and complexity of a land as old as time and as compelling as forbidden fruit will hold visitors in thrall as perhaps no other of Epcot's extraordinary movies.

After watching such a film, a quiet stroll sounds like a good idea. Upon exiting through the rear of the theater, you find yourself in a street typical of Shanghai or Peking. The street's buildings, of course, are facades, and one long facade screens what later will become Epcot's most ambitious shopping area: eight thousand square feet of Chinese merchandise, ranging from woven baskets to the finest jade. The variety and quality of the goods will make this a shopper's paradise, whether your budget is five dollars or ten thousand.

From here, you might seek out the art gallery glimpsed from the pre-show area, or take a picture in front of the tall, thin pagoda near a reflecting pool, or meander through a garden and contemplate a good Chinese dinner.

The dinner won't be ready for you at the time of Epcot Center's opening—the Chinese restaurant is planned as a future addition. But a spot of contemplation will help you to absorb the amazing sights and sounds you have experienced here, and the inner serenity it induces may be the most valuable item you'll carry away with you.

United Kingdom

It begins and ends with a pub, the United Kingdom pavilion, a happy reaffirmation of the wit and wisdom of Sydney Smith, who wrote over a century ago, "What two ideas are more inseparable than beer and Britannia?" Let's drink to that with a pint of bitter before venturing out in the midday sun for a leisurely amble through the United Kingdom of World Showcase. Besides, the pub is irresistible. Ideally situated on the bank of the lagoon, it beckons to the arriving and departing guest with all the charm and warmth of a familiar old friend.

Never been to Britain? No matter. All the world loves a pub, and the pavilion's designers have captured the spirit of this British institution, adding a little touch of Dickensian charm. But more than that, the Rose and Crown is a mini-history of the pub, an easy stroll through time as you move from the front door to the rear rooms of the establishment.

The exterior and interior of the pub have been skillfully designed in a progression of styles. From the street, you see an early cottage cheek by jowl with a Tudor tavern. This changes into a rather elegant Victorian bar on the lagoon. After entering through the cottage portion of the building, you go through an interior reflecting the same progression of styles. Many of the period details might be lost on a casual visitor without an interest in history, but the feel of the different ages will be unmistakable.

In its beginnings, the pub was a corner of somebody's home where drinks were dispensed. It evolved into a place where one could feel at home, then became a place that was a bit more than homey, and finally, in its present state, a place one would go to escape from home.

Whatever the period, a pub's decoration has always reflected the taste of the publican, the man and/or woman who operates it—usually the

The Rose and Crown, left, is one jolly little corner that will forever England be. Visitors discover here why pubs are a favorite British institution. In the rendering at right, the United Kingdom's cheery lights are reflected in the lagoon.

ROSE & CROWN

DOMINUS VOBISCUM

BASS EXPORT

English pubs are justly celebrated, and the United Kingdom pavilion will offer one that combines the best of all of them.

"guv" and his wife. The place is filled with their personal knickknacks, a quirky scattering of trophies, perhaps, or stuffed game, photographs of family members or soccer teams. It's their living room, their trophy room.

It is possible to tour the United Kingdom by walking through the shops up one side of High Street and down Tudor Lane without once stepping outside, savoring the flavor of Britain just from the interiors, so painstaking has been the designers' work. High Street, Tudor Lane, and Upper and Lower Regency streets are lined with stores and more stores. It is not without justification that the United Kingdom has been called a nation of shopkeepers.

And what a collection of shops to browse through! On the left corner of High Street as you leave the pub is a Cotswold cottage, resembling Anne Hathaway's in Stratford-upon-Avon. Half-timbered, with a thick thatched roof and a picturesque brick shed at one end, it is typical of sixteenth-century cottages in rural England.

Continuing along High Street to Tudor Lane, your way takes you, from building to building, through a broad sampling of British merchandise —from simple biscuits to luxurious Royal Doulton china. The wares become increasingly sophisticated (and expensive) as you advance. At the same time, as you go from one shop to the next, you are moving through a range of English architectural styles. Again, take note of the studied but easy flow from style to style, observable not only in the furnishings of each building but in the designs of the ceilings, the walls, even the floors. The designers' interpretation of the pavilion fairly bubbles with the idiom of their trade, a vocabulary of lintel and listel, ogee and oriel, cornice, colonnade, and cartouche.

For some it will be an education, but for most of us who don't know an astragal from an elbow joint, it all seems to be done with mirrors. How else to account for the fact that behind the High Street shops is an entirely different village with its own cozy court and common, its own grouping of buildings, its own identity? Common sense tells you that it is a new set of facades built on the backs of the High Street structures, but imagination tricks you into accepting it as another part of the kingdom.

Wherever you've roamed, both the high road and the low road lead to Britannia Square—not exactly a village green, but rather one of those lovely verdant rectangles that punctuate a stroll through almost any section of London. There's a statue, of course; there always is. And who rates this place of honor? "We considered a few kings and queens, but they didn't quite take root on American soil," says one of the designers.

Lord Nelson held a commanding lead for a day or two, but he drew some cross fire, because a military man seemed out of place in such a serene setting. Images of the poets Lord Byron and Robert Burns were contemplated, until the spotlight fell on William Shakespeare, the most widely read and highly esteemed British writer. He poses proudly above Ben Jonson's appraisal, inscribed on the pedestal: "He was not of an age, but for all time!" Behind the Bard of Avon is a lovely traditional gazebo modeled after the one in Hyde Park, a perfect spot for a band concert or even a scene or two from a Shakespearean play.

On the opposite side of the green the street is residential. It has a touch of Belgrave Square, a touch of Bedford Square, and a touch of nostalgia—the sort of place you'd love to stay on your next visit to London. Each of the Late Georgian row houses is two stories high, with dormered attics, column-framed entry, and chimneys. A railed balcony runs across the front of all, binding them together.

There's a charming view from the row houses. One side of the square remains open, the future site of a show still being created by the Imagineers. Early in the planning there was talk of a tour presentation, to be housed in an old English railroad station. The idea metamorphosed into an

A wonderfully representative group of shops offers a wide variety of popular British merchandise including Scottish cashmeres, biscuits, menswear, and elegant Royal Doulton china. This is an early version of the sign for the china shop, which is now called The Queen's Table.

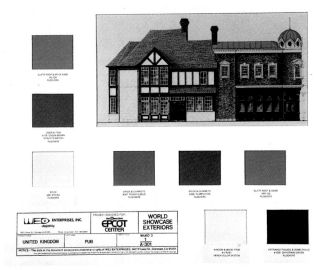

The colorboard, above, for one of the facades of the Rose and Crown illustrates the careful attention to detail that resulted in the faithful recreation of this bit of England.

High Street, left, offers a colorful mix of English architectural styles—Elizabethan, Tudor, and Victorian. But it is the Cockney "Pearlies" whose music and dancing enliven the street scene.

This delicate but beautifully detailed model is made of paper. One of the first models constructed for this pavilion, it shows an early concept of the United Kingdom and indicates the extraordinary amount of inspired handwork that went into the making of Epcot Center.

Elizabethan-type dinner theater, from which it evolved into a Victorian music hall. That's where it now stands—if a genius can be found to successfully bowdlerize the rough-and-tumble British vaudeville style for a family audience.

Resuming your stroll down the other side of Tudor Lane to High Street, you will find that the sponsor of the elegant shop inside the row houses is Pringle of Scotland, purveyors of woolens and tartans made into kilts, argyle socks, cashmere sweaters, jackets, tams, scarves—some of the United Kingdom's most practical luxuries.

A men's gift shop, His Lordship, is next, a store whose merchandise is displayed in a baronial setting decorated with coats of arms, escutcheons, crests, and heraldic trappings. You will feel posi-

tively noble just browsing there. The inviting interior includes a Great Hall—well, a smallish Great Hall—and a Jacobean room that are worth ogling even if you're not in the mood for buying.

Better save what you can for the Toy Soldier next door. Here it will be difficult to pry the children away from all the specially lighted displays of beautifully crafted British toys. Try diverting their attention to the heraldic crests worked into the shopwindows, a ploy that might well turn into a guessing game for the Anglophile: each building displays a different set of crests from colleges, the orders, major cities, and the patron saints.

Crests of the four regions of the United Kingdom—England, Scotland, Northern Ireland, and

Wales—are emblazoned on the facade of the Toy Soldier complex that fronts the lagoon. This tidy miniature palace with turrets and crenelation and the great cartouche, an elaborate coat of arms above the door, was inspired by the old part of Hampton Court, Henry VIII's favorite dwelling.

Alongside the palace is an equally tidy formal British garden, framed by low, squared-off hedges, and divided by flagstone paths. One of the paths leads to a final structure, unusual if only because it defies the architectural axiom "form follows function." It looks a little like the porch of St. James's Palace, but actually it's the restrooms.

Ending at the pub where you began your tour, you might stop there again, this time for a stirrup cup. While you drink it, contemplate the hand-painted sign. "Otium Cum Dignitate," it reads, a motto appropriate to a British pub, but perhaps to all of Epcot Center as well: "Leisure with Dignity."

The British have been called "a nation of shopkeepers" and, fittingly, their pavilion offers a broad array of their wares: tea, biscuits, china, woolens, toys, and men's clothing are a few of the temptations.

Africa

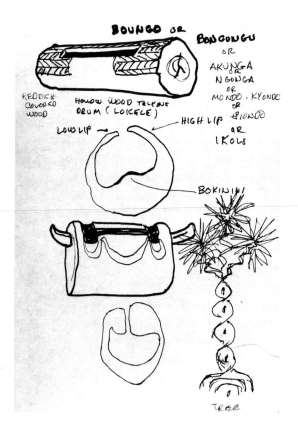

Incredible fidelity is achieved as a result of careful homework done on every detail of a presentation. These rough sketches for a display on the history of the drum, the pre-show to "The Heartbeat of Africa," document several instruments.

There is an ever-expanding number of pavilions to be incorporated into the World Showcase complex, some already in the planning stages.

Farthest along in concept is the African Nations pavilion, unique among World Showcase projects in that it is not devoted to any single country but to all of those in Africa that lie, roughly, across the equatorial belt.

The pavilion will offer a comprehensive view of the "dark continent." Its architectural motif is a tree house, in which visitors will overlook a jungle water hole in a simulated nighttime environment. The illusion of the jungle will be heightened by a remarkably authentic diorama of trees, vines, boulders, and rushing water; even the scents of the forest will be re-created. These actual objects, sounds, and smells are blended skillfully with a rear-projected film of animals visiting the water hole to convince visitors that they are actually in the heart of Africa.

One of the pavilion's shows is called "The Heartbeat of Africa." In the pre-show area, dedicated to the history of the drum, an African narrator and actual instruments vividly demonstrate its significance to the African culture.

When the Africa pavilion opens, visitors will be enthralled by the film sequence of animals coming to drink at a jungle water hole. Its effectiveness is due in large part to the painstaking thoroughness that went into the planning of the shot. Above right is the layout, and below it is the rendering; in the pavilion the experience itself awaits you.

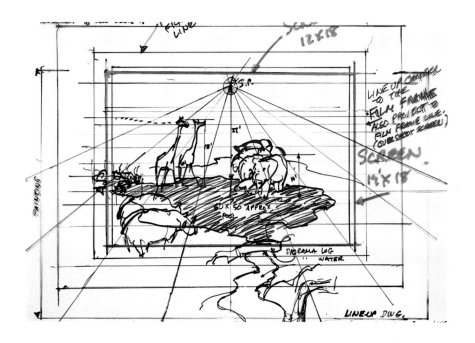

221

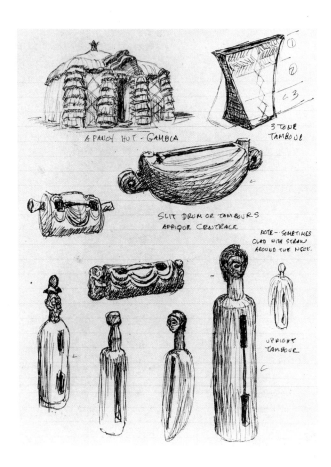

A variety of drums and African percussion instruments—even a hut in Gambia—are sketched here and on the following page.

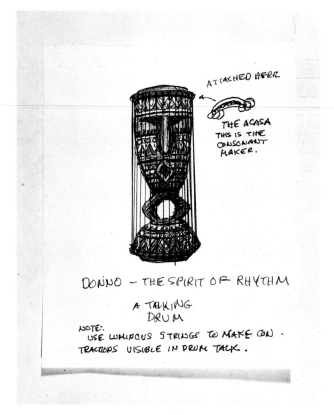

The show itself will trace the history of Equatorial Africa—its past, its present, and a glimpse of its future—through the eyes of a traditional griot, or storyteller. The filmed presentation will be not only an engaging entertainment but also a learning experience. The show will culminate with an outdoor jazz concert filmed in a modern African city, the excitement building up as superimposed laser images begin to emanate from the instruments themselves, producing abstract visual interpretations of the music that was created by slaves in America torn from their native Africa. The laser show eventually takes over the finale, forming shapes and patterns uniquely African.

In the Heritage area, an African village that is an amalgam of the styles of various countries and regions will give the visitor a broad general experience of the daily life of the African. Authentically traditional performers, in a live demonstration, will present their cultural heritage as the area's entertainment. A museum is planned to house a permanent exhibit of fine African art, with additional sculptures and paintings occasionally loaned by various African countries.

A second show, "Africa Rediscovered," will be a key attraction of the pavilion. A pre-show area, dominated by a large relief map of the continent, will graphically and entertainingly limn the geography of Africa, its flora and fauna, climate, and other information of interest.

The show, on film, will be hosted by Alex Haley, author of *Roots*, who has acted as adviser

In the Heritage area, authentic traditional performers vividly enact village life in Equatorial Africa.

to the pavilion. The film tells the story of the various kingdoms and civilizations of Equatorial Africa, a thrilling account of which the Western world is largely ignorant.

After the show, on the way out of the pavilion, the visitors will view a montage, in the style of the popular and provocative "Family of Man" exhibit, of thousands of extraordinary photographs of African people.

In a kiosk outside the exhibit, books and pamphlets will be available for purchase by those who wish to pursue the study of the history, traditions, and people of this vast and fascinating continent.

Mexico

Can any country under the sun be as rich in lore as Mexico? Was there ever a past as tumultuous, a present as colorful, a future as promising? The possibility will seem remote after a tour through the Mexico pavilion.

Epcot's Mexico, quite literally a labor of love, is unique among World Showcase pavilions in several respects:

- Except for an informal café on the lagoon and the towering pyramid that is the pavilion's architectural theme, the entire area is enclosed.

- A major part of the story of Mexico is told through the medium of the dance, a device as engaging as it is unusual.

- Most of the pavilion's design and staging crew are Mexican-Americans, whose pride in their heritage is mirrored in their presentation.

Although the excursion through "Las Tres Culturas de México" inside the pavilion is the highlight of the presentation, the signature and symbol of Mexico is the imposing pyramid temple at the entrance. Rising thirty-six feet above the lagoon in a series of steps, the structure combines elements of ancient Mesoamerican civilizations that go back to the third century A.D.

Flanked by outsize serpents' heads, which guard the temple, a steep flight of stairs leads up to the

The entrance to Mexico's pavilion is through this towering Mayan pyramid that seems to have stood here for centuries.

The face of Mexico from the lagoon, above, is warm and welcoming, although the pyramid temple at right hints at mysteries within.

Designers, below, ponder the layout of Mexico in a cutaway model of the pavilion, which will have an interior plaza and a boat ride through the country's history.

As visitors approach the entrance to the ride-through attraction, they will pass this large Olmec head, right. The Olmec culture is considered the "mother culture" of ancient Mexico.

sanctum of the high priests, whose skills in mathematics, astronomy, and other sciences were unequaled among pre-Columbian cultures.

A carved stela at the foot of the steps serves a threefold purpose: it is decorative, it houses the lights that illuminate the pyramid at night, and it effectively discourages curious children from climbing the stairs to test the will of the gods. Entrance through the pyramid to the large interior plaza beyond is by way of a museum of artifacts of Mexico's civilizations.

Above the exit from the pyramid is the monumental Sun Stone, or so-called Aztec Calendar, a marvel of intricately carved hieroglyphics indicating the days and months and illustrating the order of the cosmos. Passing beneath the calendar and between models of two colossal

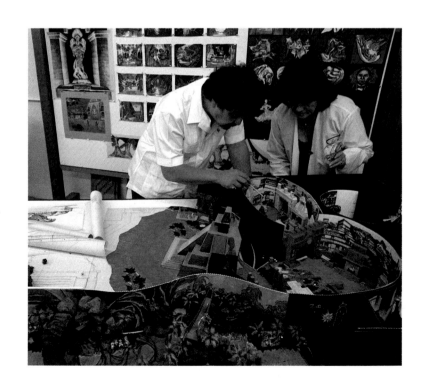

On the pre-Columbian section of the ride, visitors will encounter this Mayan high priest.

Toltec warriors, we find ourselves on the hillside terrace of a mayoral residence of a typical Mexican town.

In the twilight, we enjoy the vista over a gentle slope, across a bustling plaza, past an "outdoor" restaurant to a small lagoon that is both entrance to the ride and focal point of the panoramic view—all of this, incredibly, is indoors!

The plaza is lined on two sides with shops like those found in almost any Mexican village or town, although the designers took their example from Taxco, one of Mexico's most beautiful old settlements. In Colonial buildings with flower-decked wrought-iron balconies, tile roofs, hand-painted signs, and outdoor staircases, visitors may browse or buy jewelry, sombreros, dresses, serapes, silver goods, and other souvenirs. Strolling mariachis play their way among street vendors whose gaily decorated stands exhibit typical items offered in Mexican plazas on market day: wicker-work, vivid paper flowers, sandals, leather goods.

Authentic Mexican fare is served on the terrace and in the indoor dining room operated by the San Angel Inn, a well-known restaurant built in what is now a suburb of Mexico City.

At night the plaza takes on the atmosphere of a typical Mexican village with outdoor vendors and strolling mariachis adding to the gaiety.

From the dining terrace or from the plaza, visitors are treated at regular intervals to the spectacle of light-and-sound shows, centering on the small lagoon. Across the water is a panoramic setting with another pyramid, ancient and crumbling; a large stone Olmec head overgrown with jungle vines; grass huts, trees, shrubs, rocks; and a giant cyclorama featuring a smoldering volcano. The shows, enlivened by special effects (thunder, lightning, scudding clouds), revolve around the legends of Mexico. A favorite is the enchanting Mayan myth—at once chilling and exuberant —of how the gods wrested the gift of music from a jealous sun and bestowed it upon an Earth starved for song.

"Life was all music from that time on," concludes the legend. This seems to be borne out in the ride-through attraction, "Rio de Tiempo" (River of Time). Decorated boats cross the lagoon, cruise through an opening in the pyramid, and embark on a festive journey through Mexico's polychromatic past and uninhibited present, in which the country's songs and dances play an important part.

This is the excursion through "The Three Cul-

A beautifully executed drawing of a character from Mexico's early history seen in the ride-through.

On a sound stage at Walt Disney Studios, the dance of "The Four Elements"— Earth, Wind, Fire, and Water—is filmed for the ride-through attraction.

A dancer costumed as the Spirit of Water in "The Four Elements" has her makeup put on.

tures of Mexico"—the pre-Columbian culture, the Spanish-Colonial culture, and modern Mexico. The approach to a splendid evocation of the three major pre-Columbian civilizations—Mayan, Toltec, and Aztec—is through a "time tunnel" in which murals that range from old and faded to fresh and vivid depict Mexico's early history. At the end of the tunnel, the stone likeness of a Mayan high priest magically comes alive to bid us welcome to his city.

The city, a marvel of aesthetics and engineering, provides a dramatic setting for a number of vigorous, stylized dances portraying the astonishing accomplishments of the three great civilizations. The dancers, in beautiful, ornate period costumes, have been filmed in one-minute loops that continually replay. Although the boats move slowly, it will be impossible to absorb more than a fraction of the dances, yet they are sure to leave a lasting impression and a desire to return and see more.

The first of the dances, "Nature and Science," pays tribute to the ancients' acknowledgment of the interrelationship between man and his universe. Another, "Mathematics and Astronomy," hints at the Mayas' incredible sophistication in these demanding disciplines. The Mayas used "zero" in their calendar, the first people to have grasped the abstruse concept.

The Quetzalcóatl and Tezcatlipoca sequence

These sketches of the costume for the Spirit of Water, above, detail the goddess's elaborate headdress. A headdress for a different scene is fitted on the dancer at right.

233

The sketches opposite and below are for the dance that shows the struggle between Quetzalcóatl, who represents good, and Tezcatlipoca, the god of evil. The Aztec warriors at right—Eagle, Bear, and Jaguar—dance out a story.

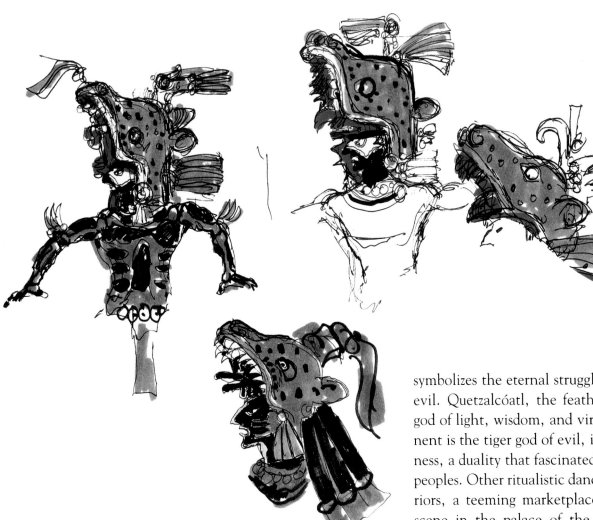

symbolizes the eternal struggle between good and evil. Quetzalcóatl, the feathered serpent, is the god of light, wisdom, and virtue, while his opponent is the tiger god of evil, ignorance, and darkness, a duality that fascinated the pre-Columbian peoples. Other ritualistic dances depict Aztec warriors, a teeming marketplace, and a portentous scene in the palace of the fabled Aztec ruler, Moctezuma II, who lost Mexico to Spain.

The arrival of the Spaniards and the subsequent rape of an entire civilization is portrayed so

235

HEAD SWIVELS
SIDE TO SIDE.

PANTS ROLLED
UP TO THE KNEE.

BODY WILL
TWIST AT THE
WAIST-SIDE
TO SIDE MORE.

LOOSE BAGGY
PANTS-
WIDE BOTTOMS

236

subtly as to be the mere whisper of a hint —Moctezuma contemplating the fall of a comet that foretells disaster to his people. The portion of the ride that follows reflects the indomitability of the Mexican people.

With the population now half Spanish, half Indian, we move into the Colonial period, presented as a kaleidoscope of doll-sized Audio-Animatronics figures in regional folk costumes, dancing, singing, and playing music. The fiestas of Mexico are celebrated in a glorious gambol that seems to embrace us all in its exuberance.

The third of "Las Tres Culturas" is modern Mexico. Presented in three-dimensional sets as well as on film are the resort areas, the cities of the 1980s, the progress of the increasingly cosmopolitan country that is the United States's good neighbor to the south.

The delightful "Festival of Children" represents Mexico's Colonial period. On the opposite page, above, are sketches of the performers; below them is a model of the Band a la Sinoloa in the Fiesta Area, scaled at 1" to a foot. A designer adjusts a figure in the small model of the Fiesta Area, above, while the full-sized set rises behind him.

Colorful lighting dramatizes the small Mayan pyramid, where visitors
board the ride-through boats, giving a foretaste of splendors to come.

But it is the nation's rich past that has most captivated the Mexican-Americans who contributed to the show so unsparingly, and who summed it up so well. "We found out much about the history, the people: the mother culture of the Olmecs; then the Mayas, who were our equivalent of the Greeks; the Toltecs, our Etruscans; the Aztecs, our Romans. And then, to be able to communicate the whole story through music, dancing, color, and texture—a universal language... We hated to see it end."

"We hated to see it end." Visitors to Epcot, after touring Future World and World Showcase, are likely to echo those words. They will also come away with something of the feeling so aptly expressed by Walter Cronkite:

This universality of Disney carries on after his death, and continues in projects that he had put on the drawing board before he died. Epcot Center in Florida is a case in point—bringing together representatives of international industry, international commerce, and the governments of other countries in a permanent world's fair. It perpetuates that theme of his that we are indeed one people.

This book is dedicated to, and inspired by, Walt Disney's vision of a world where human freedom, enterprise, and imagination combine to create an international community of people and ideas, fact and future, probable and possible, challenge and choice.

Walt Disney's Epcot chronicles a twenty-year dream, now come true through the unique blending of Disney talents—artist and designer, engineer and technician—with hundreds of advisors and consultants and thousands of construction workers. All have invested their abilities—and more than 25 million hours from dream to reality—in Walt Disney's concept. May Epcot forever be a source of joy, inspiration, hope and new knowledge to those who come here from across America and around the world.